STUDIES IN MINISTRY AND WORSHIP

studies in catholic & LITURGICAL protestant developments RENEWAL on the continent

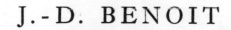

J.-D. BENOIT

STUDIES IN MINISTRY AND WORSHIP

An ecumenical forum for the discussion of the problems involved in the worship, life, and the mission of the Christian Church, and particularly for the presentation of fresh approaches that have been tested by at least some practical experience.

The General Editor is Dr G. W. H. Lampe, Edward Cadbury Professor of Theology in the University of Birmingham.

already published

WHAT IS LITURGICAL PREACHING? by R. H. Fuller

THE CHURCH'S UNDERSTANDING OF ITSELF: A Study of Four Birmingham Parishes by R. H. T. Thompson

THE MINISTRY OF THE WORD by R. E. C. Browne

CHRIST OUR PASSOVER: The Liturgical Observance of Holy Week by John T. Martin

LITURGICAL RENEWAL: Studies in Catholic and Protestant Developments on the Continent by J.-D. Benoit

HEALING AND SALVATION: An investigation of Healing Miracles in the present day by Dorothee Hoch

THE ORDINATION OF WOMEN TO THE PRIESTHOOD by M. E. Thrall

forthcoming titles

CONFESSION by Max Thurian

WHAT IS CHRISTIAN GIVING? by Brian Rice

STUDIES IN MINISTRY AND WORSHIP

EDITOR: PROFESSOR G. W. H. LAMPE

LITURGICAL RENEWAL

Liturgical Renewal

STUDIES IN CATHOLIC AND PROTESTANT DEVELOPMENTS ON THE CONTINENT

J.-D. BENOIT
*Professor of Theology
in the University of Strasbourg*

SCM PRESS LTD
56 BLOOMSBURY STREET
LONDON

Translated by Edwin Hudson from the French
First published 1958

Printed in Great Britain by
The Camelot Press Ltd., London and Southampton

52135

CONTENTS

FOREWORD

In the summer of 1956 I had the privilege of presiding over a conference of French pastors and Anglican priests at Lambeth. Although the members were enjoying the hospitality of the Archbishop of Canterbury there was nothing official or formal about the gathering; it was merely intended to allow an opportunity for mutual discussion on matters of common interest to our churches. To open up subjects for consideration a number of papers were read, some of which are now given more permanent form in this volume. There were no interpreters but each member was expected to speak his own tongue. That explains why Professor Benoit's papers have had to be specially translated. We can congratulate ourselves that the remarkable ease of the translation has allowed the elegance of the author's Gallic diction to come through unstrained.

These papers are noteworthy not merely as a literary exercise but even more for the knowledge and spirit they display. They represent the first considerable entry, since the Reformation, of French Protestant liturgiology into the field of English studies. Most readers will be astonished to learn of the wonderful revival, within the reformed churches of France and Switzerland, of the Eucharistic spirit. It is not simply that the reform of the liturgy has brought the form of worship nearer to the classical models of antiquity, but that the ultimate psychological effect of the Eucharist is said to be the same for the Protestant as for the Roman. No attempt is made to disguise the great gap that still divides the two doctrinal systems, but it is shown how in the two camps progress in liturgical adaptation, particularly in the use of the dialogue form, is proceeding on converging lines. Even in the more purely intellectual sphere there is a readiness on the part of the writer to accept the importance of tradition to an extent that is as fresh as it is refreshing.

7

It hardly needs to be said that there will be found here some things that will appear unusual to the normal Anglican. The statement that the Holy Spirit acts upon us and not upon the elements, and that the bread and wine have nothing to do with God's action will seem strange to our ears and reveal how far we are from unanimity. But there are compensations. If the Anglican manner of life with its daily round of public worship seemed alien to our visitors, most of us were surprised on our part to find how deeply the revival of community life had already become embedded in Gallic Protestantism.

It is to be hoped that the publication of this most interesting volume will help to extend the cordial good-will that animated our very rewarding conference.

✠ WM. WAND

THE EUCHARIST:
A SACRAMENT OF UNITY

SOME time ago I had occasion to take part in a retreat for deaconesses—women who, as nurses, sick-visitors, parochial assistants, teachers of backward children or of children in moral danger, had dedicated themselves whole-heartedly to the service of Christ in their fellows.

The retreat ended with a celebration of the Lord's Supper. It was most moving to see all those women in their floating white veils kneeling devoutly in prayer in the dim light of their chapel. Without distinction of denomination—members of the Reformed Church, Lutherans and Methodists—all had come together to receive the bread and wine, and in living communion with Christ to renew the consecration of their lives to his service.

For surely Christ was there. The peace of that holy place and the light that shone in those women's eyes witnessed to his presence. It was indeed he who was feeding their hearts and rekindling in them the flame of their consecration. If he were not there, where would they have found the strength to make that complete offering of their lives, and to whom would they have made the offering? Through and beyond the words, the ritual, and the hymns, they were discovering the realities which words can never fully express. They were communing with Christ, entering into the inexpressible and glorious knowledge of Christ in us.

In imagination I pictured a Communion of Carmelites or of Little Sisters of the Poor. In this domain of the living realities, on this level deeper than that of discursive thought, where in the innermost of our being Christ makes his dwelling, was that not the same communion with the same Christ? The same source of strength, the same offering of their lives to his service either in intercession or in action, but always in charity?

But I had no need to rely solely on my imagination. A few

days after taking part in the deaconesses' retreat I was present at the Mass of the Holy Spirit, sung in Strasbourg Cathedral in connection with a university celebration. There I saw communicating together professors, lecturers and students, both men and women; and I confess that I was moved by their fervour and their concentration as they waited in prayer to receive him who was coming to them and giving himself to them.

It is always like that. Wherever the Eucharist is celebrated, and the hallowed words are spoken: 'This is my body which is given for you. . . . This is my blood, the blood of the new covenant, which is shed for the remission of sins,' wherever Christians draw near with faith to receive the bread and wine (or the Host), there is Christ in the midst of them, and it is with him that they communicate.

It is on that level, the level of true piety, of the inner life of the soul, that I wish to make this study. It is not, as the reader will realize, the level of ideas, of doctrine or dogma, of intellectual discussion or theological polemic, but rather the level of concrete living, of our personal relationship with Christ, of that intimacy of the heart with him by which we can say, with St Paul: 'I live, yet not I, but Christ liveth in me.'

I am aware that the distinction between the sphere of thought and that of life is by no means an easy one to make. Although distinct, they have a certain interrelation, since life influences thought, and thought is one of the determining factors of life. Thus, if the believer habitually directs his thoughts towards the sufferings and the Passion of Christ, his religion tends to become sombre and serious, and more legalistic than that of a person whose mind is always filled with the joy of the Resurrection. Perhaps this is one of the reasons for the difference in outlook between Western Christianity, in which all of us have our roots, and Eastern Christianity. The latter is possibly less profound, not having sounded the depth of the tragedy of sin, but it seems to surpass us in the Paschal joy with which it is impregnated: 'Christ is risen! He is risen indeed!'

I am aware too—and this is doubtless due to the infirmity of our finite minds—that we are never capable of seeing more than one ray of the eternal light of truth; so that our religion is influenced by this limited view. We make it the centre of our thinking, and allow our religion to be coloured by this one ray, isolated from the full spectrum of the light of the Gospel. Doubtless our Christian life would be richer, fuller and more harmonious if we could see the whole spectrum instead of just one part of it. But who can do so? What church, what theology is capable of it? Can we really weigh up Jesus Christ, walk all round him, so to speak, looking into the innermost depths of his being and measuring his charity? Not even the gaze of the angels themselves can plumb those depths.

And yet this fragment of the truth—and how fragmentary it often is!—does lead us to the whole living Christ, indivisible in his unity. That was how the woman suffering from an issue of blood met Christ, and received from him the word of salvation: 'Thy faith hath saved thee; go in peace.' All she had done was to touch from behind the hem of his garment. It is a great lesson in humility for us. For too long we, one and all, have brandished like a flag what is but a fragment torn from the seamless coat, claiming to possess the whole truth. We have seen the violet, the indigo or the red, and, illuminated by that colour alone, we have thought we were looking at the whole of the light. Hypnotized by what we have seen of the truth, we have remained blind to the truth in others, and have been the losers thereby. The fact is that we have much to learn from each other. An eminent and pious Roman Catholic bishop, who honours me with his friendship, said the same thing to me one day, adding with the humility that is characteristic of him: 'And in saying that, I do not mean only that you must learn from us. We too have something to learn from you.'

But I am straying from my point, which was simply that there are in fact two separate domains, that of intellectual apprehension and that of concrete living. However much they may overlap, they do not coincide. Differing theologies can lead to the same Christ; differing explanations of the manner of the presence of Christ in the Eucharist do not hinder the communion of all of us with the same Christ. We can feed on him just as we can feed on bread while entertaining varying views concerning the nutritive function or the chemical composition of bread, or even while having no theory about it at all.

I

It is on this spiritual level that I believe it to be possible to say that, whatever explanation we give, whatever our theories or our dogma, when we communicate we all share the same Eucharistic joy. That is the first point which I should like to stress. For all Christians—Anglican, Reformed, Orthodox or Roman—the Eucharist is a joyful mystery. It is the pledge of our redemption. That is why it fills our hearts with a holy gladness, a gladness which is attested by Christian people of every sort. To be sure, the joy does not exclude gravity or solemnity, for our redemption was not won on the cheap. Indeed, the Lord's Supper sets up anew, as it were, the Cross in our midst. The bread (or the Host) is the body of Christ that was broken for us, and by this bread that is broken we are reminded of the wounds in hands and feet, and the flesh torn by the weight of the body. The wine in the chalice is his blood that flowed from those wounds. Thus the Lord's Supper movingly represents to us Christ on the Cross, as if he were there, crucified in our midst. It tells us the cost of our redemption: 'This is what I have done for thee!' Similarly the Mass, if I understand it aright, evokes the sacrifice of Calvary. It is as if the heavens were rent asunder, and in the chancel and on the altar of the humblest country church there is reflected the liturgy of which Christ in the presence of God is the eternal liturgist. The Mass is as it were the representation in the sight of the believer of the intercession of Christ, who as long as there are men upon the earth unceasingly offers to God the body and blood of his sacrifice. He is our High Priest, who has entered the heavens, entered with his blood into the Holy of Holies for the remission of sins. This is why the Holy Communion must be a solemn thing for us: it reminds us of the cost of our redemption, it points to the Cross. But this is also why it must be joyful, for it is our salvation which it proclaims, which has always been the ground for the thanksgiving expressed in the Preface.

Creation and redemption are the two traditional themes of the Eucharistic Prefaces:

'It is truly meet and just, right and salutary to give thee thanks at all times and in all places, Almighty God, Holy and Everlasting Father, for thy work of creation and thy redeeming love.'

With the *Sanctus* and the *Benedictus* we join our voices with those of the heavenly host, sharing in the praises sung by that great cloud of witnesses: 'The whole earth is full of his glory.' We let our joy outburst: 'Blessed is he that cometh in the name of the Lord!'

While we praise God in the Eucharist for his work of creation, so also, whatever the rite we are accustomed to use, we give joyful thanks for the remission of sins. Christ's redemption of us is the ground of our gladness. Thus the Church at each celebration of the Holy Communion intones the *Agnus Dei*:

'O Lamb of God, that takest away the sins of the world,
    Have mercy upon us!
O Lamb of God, that takest away the sins of the world,
    Grant us thy peace!'

So, however divided we are, we all sing the same song, we adore the same Saviour, we give thanks for the same redemption in which we have our share. I am inclined to think that all these songs, whatever their language or source, reach God united in one great harmony of praise, the song of the children of the same Father, blessing him from every corner of the earth for the gift of his Son and his work of salvation.

Even from this one point of view alone, we can describe the Eucharist as the great sacrament of Christian unity, for wherever it is celebrated it unites Christians around the Cross of Calvary, calling forth from them the same heartfelt praise and adoration of the author of their salvation. So that, celebrated as it is throughout Christendom, it unites Christians in thanksgiving to Jesus Christ. Perhaps without their realizing it, and in spite of themselves, it unites them more than their various theologies and their differing Eucharistic dogmas divide them.

II

But the joy of forgiveness is only one element in our Eucharistic joy. There is also the joy of the presence of Christ, for the Eucharist, as well as uniting us at the foot of the Cross, also unites us in communion with the risen Lord.

The Christian cannot dissociate Cross and Resurrection. Christ's Cross is the sign of his victory, the road to his ascension to the right hand of God. We do not sing the praises of a dead Christ, but of the living Christ, resurrected and ascended, and seated on the right hand of the Father.

It is significant that in the iconography of the early Church we find only the triumphal cross. The figure of Christ did not appear, but only his monogram (the first two letters of his name inscribed in a circle) in the place where his head had rested against the wood. Usually the monogram itself would be surrounded by a crown of laurel as a sign of triumph. Or else on one of the arms of the bare cross a dove represented the soul taking flight at the moment of death, and on the other arm a phoenix, the bird which, according to legend, is reborn from its own ashes, symbolized resurrection.

The first representations of Christ on the Cross are not the naked bleeding figures of our own crucifixes, but Christ in majesty, wearing the purple robe of the Caesars, and crowned not with thorns but with the imperial crown as emperor and king. An example of this is the Saint Vou (Holy Face) of Luques, which is still today an object of particular veneration. It was only very much later, under the influence especially of St Francis of Assisi and the sentimentalism of his time, that the crucifix with its realistic and emotional representation of the sufferings of Christ became generally used. In fact, as these historical considerations show, Christian tradition did not think of the Cross without the Resurrection.

The Eucharist, then, is not simply a memorial, commemorating the last meal that Jesus took with his disciples. This is a view which is often somewhat loosely attributed to Protestantism, but one which does not do justice to our rite of the Lord's Supper. I am convinced also that it is not in accordance with the teaching of Zwingli, at least in his later years. For Zwingli, although he had to bear the anathema of Luther, did in fact hold that to the eye of faith Christ was present in the celebration of the Eucharist. There is, indeed, no branch of the Christian Church in which the Eucharist does not signify the joy of his presence.

This joy has from the very beginning characterized what the Book of the Acts calls the breaking of bread, for at that sacred meal Christ was present. It was a meal similar to that which Christ took with his disciples in the upper room on the eve of his death; similar also to the meal at the house in Emmaus, when the risen Christ broke bread with Cleopas and another disciple; and to all those other meals taken with them in the course of his ministry, when before breaking the bread he raised his eyes to heaven and gave thanks. Peter, bearing witness to the fact which had made joy the hallmark of his life, is able to say: 'We did eat and drink with him after he rose from the dead.' Thereafter when the Lord's Supper was celebrated, the resurrected Master continued to be present with his followers. They could not see him, but though invisible he was there. He was the centre of the Eucharistic *Agape*, uniting those around him. They had his promise: 'I will not leave you orphans, I will come to you.' This was the ground of their gladness—that they knew that Christ was risen and living, and that he was present with them.

That is still the reason for the joy of the Lord's Supper, that Christ comes to be in the midst of his own. He is present at the

Holy Table as he was at Emmaus and in the upper room. We too can say with Peter that we eat and drink in his presence.

So the light of Easter breaks in upon the darkness of Calvary. Death is swallowed up in life. Christ is risen, and is always returning to his own. There will come a day when he will return in glory. Meanwhile the Church acclaims him as did the crowd on the road from Bethany to Jerusalem: 'Blessed is he that cometh in the name of the Lord; Hosanna in the highest.' Our exultant cry echoes the song of the angels at his birth, for the joy of Easter and the joy of Christmas are one.

This joy belongs to us all. It unites us around the living Christ, in the same way as we are united by God's forgiveness, which is offered to all, and of which no church can claim to have a monopoly.

I have sometimes stood on a hilltop in my native Cévennes and heard the distant sound of bells floating up on the calm evening air from the valley below. At that height it was impossible to say whether the sound came from the church, or whether it was from the 'temple', as the Protestant church is called there. It did not matter. It was the voice that called the humble village-folk to prayer and reminded them of God's mercy. Christ, of whom Thomas à Kempis said in his *Imitation* that he is at once the furthest from us and the nearest to us, is also so high above us that he will not distinguish between church-bells and chapel-bells, but will hear only the one unanimous voice of his disciples singing his praise and acclaiming his presence among them.

Together we sing for joy that Christ comes, that he returns to our midst in the Eucharist, to strengthen us in our struggles, to share with us the burden of each day, to speak to us of peace when our minds are troubled, and to put the hope of eternal life in our hearts in that hour when our way seems to be entering the shadow of death. Here again we see that in spite of the barriers we have erected, the Eucharist is a sacrament of unity, joining us all in the same triumphant joy that the presence of the risen Lord gives to his Church.

III

But the joy of the Lord's Supper is more intimate even than this collective joy that is aroused by the coming of the Lord to his Church. It is the joy of the presence of Christ within us, which is attested, confirmed, and signified by the bread (or the Host) which we eat. There is here a spiritual reality of which the Lord's Supper is the sign, and more than the sign, since we all affirm (whatever our theology) that for the believer the reality is, as Calvin said, conjoined with the sign. Thus the Lord's Supper operates what it signifies; it operates in the domain of the spiritual that of which it is, in the domain of the material, a living parable. For the bread and the wine (or simply the Host) which we receive at the Holy Table become an integral part of ourselves, of our own flesh and blood. So Christ unites himself with us, becomes life of our life and soul of our soul. As Calvin put it, we pass from our own nature into his. The Lord's Supper is thus for the believer like a blood transfusion. The Spirit of Christ is transfused into our spirit, his life becomes ours, so that thereafter it is his life that dwells in us. In the simple act of eating, if we perform it with faith, there takes place a true communion of Christ with us, a communion of his Spirit with ours.

Thus in the Lord's Supper is expressed the whole mystery of the Christian life; and at the same time it is nurtured and fed: 'I live; yet not I, but Christ liveth in me.' Is not this what we all say, the way we all live? At this level of the reality of the life lived intimately with Christ—'Christ in you, the hope of glory'— is not the Eucharist the same for all of us? Does it not bring us all the same presence and the same forgiveness? Or are we to believe that the presence is conditioned by the rectitude of our conception of the manner in which Christ is present, so that if we represent it incorrectly to ourselves there is no real presence but only an illusion? Obviously that is to attach too much importance to our explanations. That is how the Lord's Supper, which was in the mind of Christ the sacrament of the unity of all in him ('That they may be one'), has in history become the apple of discord of Christendom. And the reason is that men have tried to explain the mystery, to rationalize it by enclosing it in a formula, when what was necessary was only to be silent and adore.

In this desire to grasp the spiritual reality otherwise than by faith, to imprison it in our reasonings and our systems, in a word, to explain it (as if we ever could explain the action and the presence of God!), some have come to speaking of transubstantiation, and the Lutherans have spoken of consubstantiation, the substance of the flesh and blood being superposed upon that of the bread and wine; and the Calvinists have thought to be more faithful to the fact of Christ's Ascension, understood in a literal sense, by speaking of the localization of the Body of Christ in some specific place in the empyrean, so that it is through the intervention of the Holy Spirit that we partake by means of the bread and wine of the flesh and blood and Christ.

It is not that I do not respect and admire all this theological study, representing as it does the effort of many generations of Christians to understand the mystery better, to express in words the inexpressible. No doubt it has been a useful and necessary labour. The trouble is that instead of remaining united on what was essential, that which was professed and lived in common, men became divided over what was accessory. For things that were of secondary importance Christendom literally suffered fire and the sword. There was even the war of the Utraquists—as if communion in both kinds were the *sine qua non* of the presence of Christ. There have been unedifying arguments (to say the least) between Catholics and Protestants about the Mass. The unity of the Reform was broken by the Eucharistic controversies between Luther and Zwingli. Men have anathematized, excommunicated, and fought each other. The scandal continues of Christians who will eat and drink their ordinary meals together, but refuse to do so when it is Christ who invites them: 'Yes, Lord,' they say, 'I am willing to sup with thee, but not with this person or that person. I am willing, but on condition that we do not sit at the same table, and that thou shouldst only sup with me and with those who have the same theory as I have as to the manner in which thou art present with us.' In our Lord's lifetime the Pharisees and the orthodox wished to monopolize Jesus, murmuring when they saw him eating with publicans and sinners. 'With us, Lord, yes; but not with those people who compromise thee, and who do not know the favour thou bestowest on them.' Are we then to refuse to take part in the great banquet of God's Kingdom, because we shall not be associating there only with people from our own church or party? Are we to reproach Jesus because his love is too wide and inclusive, because he promises a place at that eternal feast to the Roman centurion, a pagan though a man of faith, and to many more who will come from all the corners of the earth to sit at table in the Kingdom of Heaven with Abraham, Isaac and Jacob? Shall we consent to share in that feast in such mixed company?

Our exclusiveness only succeeds in isolating us. A certain Anglican bishop was right when he said: 'Jesus assured us that he was present in the Holy Communion, but he did not choose to tell us how. Why should we wish to know more than he has told us?'

And yet, in spite of everything, arguments, divisions, exclusive meals taken at tables apart when the great family table is laid ready for all, in spite of anathemas, violence, and even the shedding of blood—and the 'damned spot' remains burning on all our hands—the Eucharist is still the great sacrament of Christian unity. Through it we are privileged still to commune with Christ, and in him, in spite of all that separates us, to commune with each other. For in so far as we truly approach him, we come closer to all those who believe in him, wherever and whoever they be. For Christ excludes no one: 'Come unto me, all ye that labour and are heavy laden.' All ye! No one is turned away who comes to him with faith.

The Eucharist is thus the trysting-place where the disciple meets his Master, joins himself to him, feeds on him. In spite of our tables divided by unscalable walls of suspicion, of prejudices, of age-old animosities, it is still the link uniting all Christian people. The bonds that join them may be invisible; they do not go directly between them, but converge on Christ to meet in him. In Christ we are one—even perhaps in spite of ourselves. If everything has not crumbled, if there is still some underlying unity in the Christian world, it is to the Eucharist that we owe it. The Eucharist remains among us as a perpetual recall to unity. It bears within itself the necessity of unity as well as being a sort of first sketch of unity, a prophecy of that unity for which Christ prayed: 'That they may be one.'

Unity in Jesus Christ is not a new ideal discovered in our own age. It could never be brought about by the efforts of our own hands. It is given. It exists by the very fact of the Eucharist, and has been there from the beginnings of Christianity. Our bloody struggles have not succeeded in destroying it. In instituting the Lord's Supper, Jesus founded for ever the unity of the Church: *Credo unam sanctam, catholicam ecclesiam!* What we must do is to become aware of this reality, too often clouded over by our polemics. We must deepen the reality of this communion with Christ so as to see more clearly that it implies communion with our brethren. If we find it difficult to overcome in a moment all the obstacles raised by our own minds and their inveterate habits of thought, we must at least enlarge our hearts and learn to love each other. For this unity in love is required by the Lord's Supper; it is implied in principle in our communion with Christ: 'By this shall all men know that ye are my disciples, if ye have love one to another.'

It is in the one Lord Jesus Christ that the Eucharist unites us. 'Is Christ divided?' asked St Paul, alluding to the factions in Corinth. Our divisions do not divide him: he is the only-begotten, the same yesterday, and today, and for ever; the same in Geneva and in Rome, in Africa and in Asia, in every clime—inseparable from his Gospel, which is one and the same for all. None can monopolize him. Our ecclesiastical barriers, the barbed wire of our intransigence and our fanaticism, are no obstacle to him. There is no door barred by our rules, our prejudices and our mutual defiance through which he cannot pass, as when on the evening of his resurrection he came into the upper room, all the doors being shut.

The reality of Christ's presence is the joy of the Lord's Supper. It goes deeper than our ideologies and anathemas. One of the most striking things about our liturgies is their unanimity when, instead of disputing, they are adoring.

Thus the Canon of the Mass: 'May thy body, O Lord, which I have received, and thy blood which I have drunk, cleave to my bowels (*adhaereat visceris meis*).' And again: 'Make me always adhere to thy commandments, and never suffer me to be separated from thee.'

The Anglican Prayer-Book: 'Grant us . . . so to eat the flesh of thy dear Son Jesus Christ, and to drink his blood . . . that we may evermore dwell in him, and he in us.'

The Scottish Liturgy: '. . . beseeching thee that all we who shall be partakers of this Holy Communion may worthily receive the most precious Body and Blood of thy Son Jesus Christ, and be . . . made one body with him, and that he may dwell in us and we in him'.

The Lutheran Liturgy: 'Be in our midst. We will welcome thee with joy. Dwell in us!'

The Liturgy of the Church of South India: 'Be present, be present, O Jesus, thou good High Priest, as thou wast in the midst of thy disciples, and make thyself known to us in the breaking of the bread.' And again: 'Grant . . . that we may evermore dwell in him and he in us.'

The Reformed Liturgy: 'Thou who knowest the hearts, purify us and renew in us the certainty of thy forgiveness and the presence of the Risen One, that he may live in us and we in him.'

The first Geneva Liturgy (1545) saw this union of Christ and the believer as the essential thing in the Lord's Supper. In the preliminary instruction Calvin wrote: 'So the chief end of the whole mystery of the Supper is that we should live in Christ and that he should live in us.' In the exhortation immediately preceding the breaking of the bread we find the words: 'Firstly, then, let us believe these promises which Jesus Christ, who is the infallible Truth, uttered with his own mouth, namely that he wishes us to partake of his body and blood, to the end that we may possess him entirely, so that he may live in us and we in him.'

Here, finally, is the litany of praise with which our Sisters of Pomeyrol[1] follow the celebration of the Eucharist:

'O Christ, thou art our way,
O Christ, thou art our truth,
O Christ, thou art our life,
O Christ, thou art in us.

O Christ, thou art the bread of life,
O Christ, thou art the vine,
O Christ, thou art the spring of living water,
O Christ, thou art in me.'

The litany continues, the refrain alternating: 'O Christ, thou art in us. O Christ, thou art in me.'

Such unanimity is moving. For all Christians without exception the Lord's Supper is essentially the token of the union of Christians with Christ. The knowledge that even communicating separately we all meet in Jesus Christ, ought to forge between us a link that is stronger than our divisions. The Eucharist, considered thus in its essentials, is indeed—in spite of appearances, and in spite of ourselves—the sacrament of our unity.

IV

Because it is communion with Christ, the Holy Communion unites us, lastly, in a common consecration and obedience.

[1] A community of women, vowed to a life of worship and intercession, whose house, in the South of France, is a centre for retreats.

Whether it is the Communion of deaconesses to which I referred at the beginning, or the Communion of the Little Sisters of the Poor, the outcome in both cases is normally the same: a life given to the service of Christ among their fellows. This service and obedience given for love of Christ constitute among us, if we have eyes to see it, the strongest of bonds, just as the soldiers of one army, under the orders of one leader who is loved equally by all, feel themselves bound together.

In order to unite us in obedience, the Eucharist unites us first in love of Christ. Love is the condition of all union with him. 'If a man love me,' Jesus said, 'he will keep my words: and my Father will love him, and we will come unto him, and make our abode with him.' These words, from St John's Gospel, say all there is to be said. They cannot fail to remind us of the Eucharist.

All there is to be said—but there is a condition: 'If a man love me . . .' What sort of a communion would it be without love?

The consequence is stated: '. . . he will keep my words'. What sort of a communion would it be without faithfulness?

A communion without love, the presence in us of one whom we did not love, would be a constraint, a burden, a continual accusation. In Sartre's play *Huis Clos*, four people are shut up together in a room with no outlet to the outside world. They are condemned to be continually in each other's presence, without ever being able to escape even for a moment. It is like a foretaste of hell. If the presence of another person is to become a joy to us, we must love that person. It follows that we can scarcely conceive of a communion without love. Indeed, would there be any communion at all? Of course one can still 'go through the motions', but where is the reality? 'If a man love me we will make our abode with him.' 'But if a man love me not,' Jesus seems to be saying, 'how could we make our abode with him?' Christ does not break doors down. He waits until we open to him; and opening to him means, firstly, loving him. Without that love any communion we imagine we have with him can only be illusory.

If truly to commune with Christ we must love him, all our

23

Eucharists, in so far as they are not empty gestures, unite us in that love. For one cannot come to the Holy Communion without saying again Peter's prayer: 'Lord, thou knowest all things; thou knowest that I love thee.'

I like to remember the words of a little Scots girl whose memory was bad and who was a little simple-minded. She had answered very badly during the preliminary examination before Communion, which in that country takes place before the elders of the Church, austere and serious-minded men, steeped to the marrow in the Bible. Clearly the attempt to get the catechism into her untutored head had failed, and it was decided that she must have another year's instruction before being admitted to Communion. The examination over, the minister found the child crouching in a doorway, the tears streaming down her face. He tried to comfort her, assuring her that another year's religious instruction would be good for her. 'It isn't that,' the girl replied, 'it's not being able to go to Communion. I did want so much to show the Lord Jesus how much I love him!' The catechism had not entered her head, but the love of Christ was in her heart. In spite of her ignorance she knew more about it than many who could recite their catechism from end to end, and the minister decided that she knew enough to be admitted nevertheless to Communion.

That is what the Communion is—a testimony of love, at the same time as it fosters that love in our hearts And that love, uniting us all to the living Christ, is a bond of unity between us. The more we love Christ, the nearer we shall feel to each other.

What sort of communion would it be without faithfulness?

There is a sentimental kind of love for Christ which can be dangerous if it becomes effeminate. One can swoon before the cross, and shed tears which are not always those of repentance. One can bind oneself to Christ with the bonds of an almost carnal love, and neglect the humble tasks of daily life in order to indulge in mystical contemplation. There can thus be in our love for Christ an element which still wallows in the mud of sensuality. But Christ desires only a love that is made of faithfulness: 'If a man love me, he will keep my words.' It is in this faithfulness that love is manifested; and there is no love without it. 'He that hath my commandments, and keepeth them, he it is that loveth me.' Only that love is authentic which expresses itself in what Vinet called a servitude of love.

This is not to say that the yearning of the heart is valueless, or that Christianity excludes in principle the ardour of contemplation and the fervour and intimacy of mysticism; but contemplation and fervour must lead to obedience and be consummated in obedience, otherwise there is no true union with Jesus Christ.

It is obvious. What after all am I? What, essentially, is it that constitutes the living being? It is will, desire, or at least tendency, movement, choice. It is therefore impossible to conceive of a communion with Christ that leaves me autonomous, that does not include my will, which is fundamental to me. We cannot be united to him with all our being if our will remains a stranger to him, in revolt against his will. All unions other than the union of obedience are superficial and illusory. Every testimony of love, every tremor of emotion, and even the acceptance by the mind of all the articles of faith, signify very little so long as our will is not in unison with the will of God revealed in Jesus Christ. 'Obedience,' Vinet said, 'is the union of the creature with the Creator.' That is to say, the union of the Creature and the Creator is accomplished and completed only in obedience.

Obedience to God's will means the sacrifice of what is dearest to us, our independence; it is in fact a sort of abdication of ourselves. It is precisely this sacrifice which all the Eucharistic liturgies demand of us. With a sure intuition they have recognized that union with Christ implies renunciation of self, alignment of our will with his, the sacrifice of our bodies—that is to say of the whole of ourselves—apart from which, as the apostle says, there is no 'reasonable service'.

Pope Pius XII solemnly affirms the same thing in the Encyclical *Mediator Dei*: The faithful, he says, offer themselves 'as a spiritual victim with and through the High Priest himself. . . . We thus identify ourselves with Christ as victim for the greater glory of the Eternal Father.'[1] Similarly in the Anglican liturgy: 'And here we offer and present unto thee, O Lord, ourselves, our souls and bodies, to be a reasonable, holy, and lively sacrifice unto thee.' And in the Reformed Liturgy: 'We offer ourselves to thee as a living and holy sacrifice.'

Love, self-renunciation in obedience, and communion are bound up together. While love manifests its sincerity and reality only in obedience, obedience in its turn finds its driving power only in love. Without love it would be the obedience of the mercenary, forced on us by fear, full of scruples and torments of conscience.

'If a man love me,' said Jesus, 'he will keep my words.' It has a double meaning. It means that love is perfected in obedience, the obedience being the proof and the manifestation of the love. But it also means that only love makes true obedience possible. To keep his words, one must love him.

The Eucharist unites us in the same love for Christ, and in the same will to consecration and service; it unites us therefore one with another at the deepest level of our being, as soldiers of the same army, as I have said, united in the same trusting love of their leader, in the same will for the same victory, in the same offering of their lives.

This is not a unity to be made, to be organized and pursued: it is a fact; it is given to us. In instituting the Eucharist, Christ united his Church for ever on earth. He created among all his disciples a bond stronger than their divisions and their exclusiveness could ever be. Unity is there, in the Lord's Supper, in communion with him, in our common love and our common consecration, which is our humble response to the sacrifice he made for all. The Abbé Couturier once wrote: 'We must no longer approach Christian unity at the level of dogmatic concepts—they

---

[1] *Christian Worship, Encyclical Letter 'Mediator Dei' of Pope Pius XII*, translated by Canon G. D. Smith, Catholic Truth Society, London, 1947, pp. 46-7.

are an end-product, not a point of departure—but at the level of Christ in prayer, the Lord of the Church; no longer primarily as a problem requiring the exercise of the mind, but as a mystery given from on high.'

What then are we to do? Aware of this underlying unity, we should each communicate in his own church, seeking as we do so to deepen the meaning of this communion, never content with superficial communions, but going to the roots—for it is at the roots that we meet each other, like trees, separated by a high wall, which are yet joined where their roots feed on the same nourishing soil.

'Rooted in Christ,' said St Paul. It is in the measure in which we are rooted in him that we shall be able to meet each other and communicate through the roots, in the same love, the same hope, the same obedience. Then the Eucharist will be shown ever more clearly to be what it has never ceased to be since the evening of the first Supper: the sacrament of our unity in Christ.

RECENT LITURGICAL DEVELOPMENTS IN THE FRENCH-SPEAKING REFORMED CHURCHES

WE are witnessing at present a liturgical revival among the French-speaking Reformed Churches. In the last few years a whole crop of new liturgies has seen the light of day: the Liturgy of the Canton of Vaud in 1940, the Geneva Liturgy in 1946, the Liturgy of the Churches of the Bernese Jura in 1955, and lastly the Liturgy of the Reformed Church of France in 1955.

I. A BRIEF HISTORICAL SURVEY

The liturgical revival is undoubtedly long overdue. It is a fact that the Reformers, and especially Calvin, were unable to devote the necessary time and thought to liturgical questions. More urgent tasks, matters of life and death for the new movement of reform, absorbed all their energies. As far as worship was concerned, they attended to the most urgent things first. In Strasbourg there was worked out the liturgy which was to become the parent of all the liturgies in French: *La manyère de faire prières aux Eglises françoises* ('The manner of making prayers in the French Churches'). This liturgy is no more than a translation and adaptation of the Strasbourg Liturgy in German, of 1539, which was used by Bucer and was due in part to him. Calvin, when he came to the Rhenish city, retained the order of worship, merely adding the singing of the Decalogue by the congregation. As is well known, this Strasbourg Liturgy was based directly on the Mass, everything connected with the offertory being suppressed.[1]

This liturgy of the *Ecclesiola Gallica*, the little church of the French refugees of which Calvin was the pastor, had however been preceded by the liturgy attributed to Farel, printed at Serrières

[1] Cf. W. D. Maxwell, *John Knox's Genevan Service Book*, London, 1931.

29

(Neuchâtel) in 1533: *La manière et fasson qu'on tient ès lieux lesquels Dieu de sa grâce a visités* ('The manner and fashion adopted in the places which God of his grace has visited'). This liturgy is itself a fairly free adaptation of the Strasbourg liturgies. Farel, in fact, was in Strasbourg shortly before 1533, and it is not surprising that he was struck by the form of worship which was being practised there. In particular *La manière et fasson* contains in its marriage service an exhortation directly inspired by the text in use at Strasbourg. Thus in any case it was the Strasbourg liturgies which lay at the origin of the French reformed liturgies. The liturgy worked out by Calvin on his return to Geneva does no more than reproduce his Strasbourg Liturgy with certain modifications insisted upon by the Magistracy. It is this Geneva Liturgy which is the source of the whole of the Reformed liturgical tradition in France and elsewhere.

We lived for more than three centuries on this Genevan tradition, a tradition which cared little for the Church's year, and scarcely stressed at all the great Christian festivals, a tradition which has remained outside the great ecumenical current in the peculiarly sombre and polemical character of its liturgy of the Lord's Supper, a tradition centred entirely on the preaching of the Word, which thrust the celebration of the Eucharist into the background, a tradition, in short, which gave to worship a didactic intention and an essentially intellectual cast.

Certain individuals did from time to time feel the poverty of their liturgical heritage, precious though it was. Such an one was Jean Frédéric Ostervald, a pastor in Neuchâtel at the beginning of the eighteenth century. He had an ecumenical sense—rare enough at that time—and regretted the anomalous character of the Geneva Liturgy. In 1701 he wrote to his friend Turretin: 'Our adversaries are right when they say that Calvin introduced a form of worship entirely unknown to antiquity.' His liturgy (1713) is a timid enough attempt at reform, but one thing it did was to open the way to the restoration of the liturgical year in Reformed worship.

This did not prevent the Reformed Liturgy from adhering, until the end of the nineteenth century, to strictly Calvinist norms. The liturgy of the Lord's Supper in particular received only verbal modifications in order to bring its archaic language more up to date.

The real father of the modern liturgical revival was Eugène Bersier, pastor of the Etoile Church in Paris. Of Swiss origin, he had English blood in his veins through his mother, so that the Anglican liturgy was not without influence on the liturgical developments in the Reformed Church. Conscious of the poverty of the forms of prayer and the passivity of the faithful in worship, Bersier worked out a liturgy for his Etoile Church which constitutes a considerable advance. The congregation is made to take a more active part in the worship through the numerous responses required of it. There are different prayers for each Sunday of the month, and special forms for the festivals. The Eucharistic liturgy especially, although still too didactic in tone, comes back with the Preface and the *Sanctus* into the main ecumenical tradition. In 1888 Bersier continued his pioneering work by submitting a 'Liturgical Project' to the national Synod. Not many followed his lead, however. Most remained faithful to the Calvinist tradition. As regards the Eucharistic liturgy in particular, Bersier's form of service was rejected. The form of worship obtaining at the Etoile remained therefore an exception, and was for long looked upon as an Anglican enclave in the heart of the Reformed Church of France.

Among the precursors in France of the present movement mention ought to be made of Wilfred Monod, the author of several liturgical essays. One of these, the *Cérémonial des Veilleurs*, a little book for use by the Protestant 'Third Order' of the *Veilleurs*, or 'Watchers', which he had founded, contains new forms of service for the Eucharist. In his *Livre de prières* ('Prayer-book') for use by the *Veilleurs*, a sort of layman's breviary, the pastor of the Oratoire sets out to restore to Reformed worship the observation of the ecclesiastical year. Although his formularies are too personal and original for use in our services—one recognizes at once the some-what affected style and the occasionally florid imagination of their author—Wilfred Monod's work has nevertheless been a vigorous stimulus to the liturgical movement.

Parallel with what was happening in France, an analogous movement was taking place in French Switzerland. Pastor Jules Amiguet made his chapel of St John in Lausanne a veritable liturgical laboratory, as he liked to call it. With stained glass, a 'Way of the Beatitudes' taking the place of the Stations of the Cross, a choir, candles on the altar, liturgical colours, he opened, one might say, in the wall of puritanism in worship a breach that will not be closed up again.

But it is one of his followers, Pastor Richard Paquier of Saint Saphorin on the shore of the Lake of Geneva, who has given the greatest impetus to the liturgical movement in Switzerland, and consequently in France as well. He founded the 'Church and Liturgy' group, which advocates a return to the ancient forms of worship, and, especially, the reform of the liturgy of the Eucharist. Some find this movement too 'High Church', but we all owe him a great debt.[1]

In this study I shall deal more especially with the tendencies revealed in the new Liturgy of the Reformed Church of France, on which a team of theologians, including both pastors and lay-men, has been working since just after the last war, under the energetic chairmanship of Pastor Pierre Bourguet, whom I have had the honour of succeeding on his becoming head of the Reformed Church of France.

The revival which is taking place is all the more remarkable when one considers that French Protestants, by their principles as well as for historical reasons, have never taken kindly to the vast domain of liturgy; they had almost no feeling for it and it was little to their liking. The Reformation took the Word of God, the *Verbum*

---

[1] Richard Paquier is the author of a stimulating book which is in effect the manifesto of the movement: *Traité de Liturgique*, Delachaux & Niestlé, Neuchâtel and Paris, 1954.

audibile, as the basis of its doctrine and its life. In this way it pushed into the background everything of the nature of rites and ceremonies. The essential thing was the preaching of the Word, the sermon. People came to church mainly to 'receive doctrine', as Calvin put it. Hence the didactic tone of the Reformed Liturgy and of worship in general. We are faced, therefore, with a liturgical deficiency which proceeds from the general conception of worship as it was understood by the Reformers, in which, as Vinet has said, all is speech, everything is explained, everything is put into words.

Seeing the preaching of God's Word as paramount, the Reformation not only considered as secondary everything to do with ritual and ceremony, but rejected as tainted with idolatry all the outgrowths which had been added to the Word, like so many brambles preventing access to the spring of living water. It must be admitted that the liturgy had become the privileged domain of all these unscriptural superfluities. Mariolatry, the cult of the saints, Purgatory, everything that the Reformation, armed only with the sword of the Word of God, rejected and condemned, was part of the very texture of the liturgy and could not be extirpated from it. And so it was condemned in its entirety, the ecclesiastical year was abolished, and there was left for worship only an arid abridgement of the liturgy of the Mass—a mere skeleton liturgy.

The influence of the ultra-spiritualists was exerted in the same direction. The Reformation did of course react against this radical spiritualism, but in reacting it allowed itself to be influenced. What principally characterized this ultra-spiritualism was the store it set by spontaneity—such spontaneity as is exemplified by the charismatic .outbursts in the Corinthian church. It appeared to believe that only the direct outpourings of the heart could be sincere, and that if the same prayer was said twice it ceased to be inspired. Such a position was hostile to all liturgical form, and it was not without its influence on the attitude of the Reformers. Certain Free Churches and Methodists still conduct their worship with as little liturgical matter as possible: no reading of the Law, no confession of sins, no absolution, no creed, no set prayers. The only liturgical prayer admitted is the Lord's Prayer.

Then again, a liturgy imposes upon us a certain discipline. One must cast off one's own individuality and take part in a common prayer, and against this discipline Protestant individualism protests. Of course pure logic demands that such individualists should not join in common worship at all, for even in order to follow a prayer, however spontaneous and extempore, one must forsake oneself to some extent. This ultra-individualism, in fact, does not fit into the liturgy because it does not in general fit in with the Church. Church and Liturgy go together. He who is responsive only to his own mental state can never join in the great voice of the Church.

History, no less than principle, has played its part in this inadaptability to liturgical forms. Our worship was moulded by Calvin, but also by the Desert Assemblies.[1] These Assemblies had no liturgical furniture or symbols. A barn, a deserted sheep-fold, a cave, its walls dripping with moisture, a plantation of chestnut-trees—such was their sanctuary. No altar, no cross, no lights; sometimes a portable pulpit; for the Communion service, a rough plank on sticks driven into the earth, and a tin cup and plates, or even ordinary glasses begged from a friendly house. It was in this bare setting that worship took place, a worship without a liturgy. And yet the Huguenots knelt in the mud and repeated Calvin's confession, and then cried aloud: 'Have mercy! Have mercy!' In all its simplicity was that not the greatest and most moving of liturgies? It is easy to see how such assemblies, which were for a century the only form of Protestant common worship, did not develop any liturgical sense among us. When normal times returned, the great bare-walled 'temples', more like barns than churches, seemed sumptuous compared with the barns and sheep-folds in which worship had until then been carried on.

[1] *Translator's note:* Upon the revocation of the edict of Nantes in 1685, many Huguenots fled into the wilds of the Cévennes, there to continue the practice of their proscribed worship.

Add to this the influence of Huguenot Prophetism, which in any case was closely connected with the Desert Assemblies. The 'prophets of the Cévennes', as they are called, were preachers who would fall into a state of trance and pronounce impassioned discourses, generally in French—in spite of the fact that in the normal state they spoke and understood only the local *patois*. Women, girls and even children, falling under the influence of inspiration, became prophets and prophetesses. There were visions, sometimes accompanied by convulsive movements, and inflammatory invective directed against 'great Babylon' (the Roman Church), and always the loud cries of 'Have mercy!' from the assembled people. Later this prophesying became less impassioned; the prophet no longer spoke in a state of trance. But the assemblies for worship retained something of the old effervescent spontaneity which brooked no liturgical constraint.

This antipathy to discipline passed into the blood of French Protestantism, in spite of Antoine Court's reaction, and his implacable fight against the vestiges of the Prophetism of the Cévennes, which he called Illuminism. The influence of Prophetism can still be seen in certain revivalist meetings, in which even examples of glossolalia, or speaking with tongues, are occasionally found. All this is as far removed as it could well be from the reserve, the moderation, the discretion and modesty which a liturgy imposes.

Persecution itself played a part in the development of a certain antipathy to liturgical worship, which was too reminiscent of Catholicism. One understands the banishment of the crucifix from the Reformed churches when one knows that martyrs at the stake were offered an image of Christ to kiss, fixed on the end of a pole. This opposition was extended even to the plain wooden cross, and it was a revolution when at Nîmes, the headquarters of Cévennes Protestantism, it was desired to set up a cross over the pulpit.

Clearly, from the liturgical point of view, Protestantism has been in the wilderness, if one may put it so. In an outlying part of my first parish, in the Cévennes, the men-folk used to stop to talk and argue in the square, under the chestnut-trees in front of the door of the chapel-of-ease, waiting until the liturgical part of the service was over. Now and again the door would open sufficiently for me to see a head thrust discreetly inside, listening for a moment to see what part of the service we had reached. Then the door would be closed again, and the owner of the head would go back to reassure his companions: it was not time yet. Just as I was about to read from the Bible the whole phalanx of the men would tramp in. The liturgical part was over: in their eyes it was no more than a prelude, a sort of *hors-d'œuvre*. With the Bible reading, the extempore prayer and the sermon, the service was really beginning, and they began to take part. Without realizing it, they were formed in the tradition of the Desert Assemblies.

The present liturgical revival is all the more remarkable.

II. THE NEW LITURGY OF THE LORD'S SUPPER

I have no hesitation in saying that the Liturgy of the Lord's Supper in use in the Reformed Church of France up to the time of the introduction of the new Liturgy, a first draft of which appeared in 1948, was a sickly child of the Reformation. In its main lines it went back to Calvin himself, and was inspired—in parts literally—by the Geneva Liturgy. It was catechetical, sermonizing and polemical, all faults which a liturgy ought to avoid, for it is not the purpose of a liturgy to be a catechesis, that is to say an explanation of what is being done, nor a sermon, nor yet a refutation of Roman Catholic errors. All that has its place, but not in the liturgy. Add that it was sombre and joyless, dominated by the shadow of the Cross, unillumined by the light of the Resurrection. It was a Good Friday liturgy rather than an Easter one; it had nothing of the gladness of thanksgiving: it was not Eucharistic in the proper meaning of the term.

The fact was that in reacting against the Mass it had cut itself adrift from the ecumenical tradition, obstinately rejecting everything that might be reminiscent of the Roman Canon: no Preface, no *Sanctus*, no *Hosannah*, no *Agnus Dei*, nothing to remind one of the *Unde et memores* or the *Non sum dignus*. It was unlike any other form of worship, quite unrelated to the great ecumenical tradition of Christendom, like a boulder in the midst of a stream. The new liturgy represents a return to this ecumenical tradition.

1. *The Preface*. Departing completely from the traditional Genevan text, we have taken back the Preface, rejoining in this the universal Church. The most ancient Eucharistic liturgies we know consist essentially of this prayer of thanksgiving, which is like a noble doorway leading to the Communion. The Preface at all times and in all places gives thanks to God, on the one hand for his work of creation and his glory manifested in the universe, and on the other for his redeeming love. It is in line with the great Jewish prayer in honour of the God who had created the world, and who had led his people over the Red Sea, the crossing of the Red Sea having always been understood by Christians as a type of salvation.

Here, for example, are a few sentences from the oldest Eucharistic liturgy we possess, that of St Hippolytus, Bishop of Rome at the beginning of the third century:

℣. The Lord be with you!
℟. And with thy spirit.
℣. Lift up your hearts!
℟. We turn them towards the Lord.
℣. Let us give thanks to the Lord.
℟. It is worthy and right.

'We give thee thanks, O God, for thy dear Son, whom thou hast sent in these last times to be our Saviour and Redeemer, and the Messenger of thy will, who is thy inseparable Word; by whom thou hast created all things and in whom thou art well pleased; whom thou didst send from heaven into the womb of a Virgin, and who, having been conceived, became incarnate and was manifested as thy Son, born of the Holy Spirit and of the Virgin.'

Already in this early Preface we see expressed the two great grounds of our thanksgiving and adoration: the glory of God seen in his work of creation, and his work of redemption accomplished in Jesus Christ.

These two themes of creation and redemption are present in Col. 1.15-20. The suggestion has been made—not without reason —that we have here a Eucharistic prayer of the primitive Church: actually the first Preface. The language is, in fact, liturgical in style. The movement of the passage is the same as that of all the Prefaces: He who . . . In him . . . Through him . . . Thus the Preface is not only part of the great ecumenical tradition, but also goes back to the New Testament itself.

Again, as it directs our gaze towards God the Creator and Redeemer, and towards Jesus Christ in whom God has manifested his love to us, it takes our minds off ourselves, draws us away from self-analysis, over-scrupulousness, and introspection, all of them attitudes which generate anxiety and worry, filling our hearts instead with thanksgiving and joy.

We have, then, come back to the Preface, and with it to the *Sanctus* and the *Benedictus*. The Church acclaims him who comes in the name of the Lord, as the multitudes acclaimed him on the road from Bethany—the Christ who returns to his people, the Christ who is present at each celebration of the Holy Communion.

The *Hosannah* of our Eucharistic acclamation reminds us of the angels' song of praise. As on the night of his Nativity the angels accompanied with their praises the coming of the Christ to earth, so when we celebrate the Holy Communion the host of heaven joins with the Church assembled to greet the coming of the Christ among his people: 'Therefore with the universal Church, with the angels and the whole company of heaven, with the great cloud of witnesses, with one accord in gladness, we laud and magnify thy glorious Name.'

Then we are no more alone; the barriers are down; separation is ended. The poorest and humblest country church is transfigured; its walls seem to recede, and there is present around us a great invisible multitude; all heaven is singing with us.

That is the note of joy struck by the Preface. Too often the Lord's Supper is turned into something funereal. One has had the feeling sometimes of being gathered in a sort of death-watch around a cross with Christ's lifeless body still hanging on it, in a gloomy sadness on which the light of the Resurrection morning seems not yet to have dawned. It ought not to be so. The Lord's Supper should take its place among the joyful mysteries. After all, in the primitive Church it was celebrated with an overflowing joy that amounted to a sort of spiritual intoxication—the joy of the soul welcoming him who deigns to come and 'sup with it'.

All this is not to say that the Lord's Supper is not also to remind us of the Cross. When, after the great silence—'Let all mortal flesh keep silence before the Lord!'—there fall on our ears the words of the Institution: 'This is my Body which is given for you. . . . This cup is the new covenant in my Blood . . .,' how can we fail to wonder at the immensity of the sacrifice, the matchless price that had to be paid for our redemption? Nevertheless, is it not at this very point that we are filled with thankfulness for that redeeming love, a thankfulness all the warmer in view of the heavy price that was paid? Just as the Resurrection cannot be understood apart from the sombre background of Calvary, so the Cross cannot be understood apart from the glorious anticipation of the Resurrection. It is inseparable from the Resurrection. The trouble is that we bewail Christ crucified, as the women of Jerusalem did, or else we weep over ourselves, so darkening with the shadow of the Cross the bright light of Easter. That way lies a gloomy, tragic or sentimental Christianity, which stops at the sin without reaching the pardon, which dwells on man's distress rather than God's mercy, which pays more attention to what the Christian has to give up than to what he has been given, which thinks about his defeats rather than his victories, which concerns itself

39

with death rather than life. Such does not seem to me to be the Christianity of the primitive Church of the New Testament, with its shouts of victory and its songs of gladness: 'Thanks be to God, which giveth us the victory. . . . I can do all things in him that strengtheneth me. . . . In all these things we are more than conquerors.' These are fanfares of trumpets, bold challenges flung at sin, at evil, at death itself.

It is in this way that our new liturgy performs the task of bringing us back to the meaning of Christian joy and victory.

2. *The Eucharistic Prayer.* This Eucharistic prayer which follows the account of the Institution is short. It expresses in the first place our response to the love of Christ for us, supremely manifested in the Holy Communion: 'My body given for you.' Our response can only be the consecration and offering of ourselves: 'We offer unto thee ourselves as a living and holy sacrifice.' This sacrifice of ourselves, which St Paul calls a 'reasonable service'—that is to say logical, consequential—takes the place of the Offertory of the Roman Liturgy, so that in this the Reformed Liturgy diverges from that of the Mass.

In fact the Reform has from its very beginning always suppressed the Offertory as understood in the Mass, affirming that the true 'offertory' required of us is the offering of ourselves.

At the time of the first Evangelical service of worship in German at Strasbourg, on the 16th February, 1524 (twelve years before the publication of the first edition of Calvin's *Institutio Christianae religionis*, whose author was then only fifteen years old), Theobald Nigri (or Schwartz) substituted for the Offertory of the Mass the following invitation to prayer: 'Dear brothers and sisters, let us pray God the Father by our Lord Jesus Christ, that he will send us the Holy Spirit, the Comforter, to make our bodies a living sacrifice agreeable to God, which is the reasonable service that is pleasing to God. May he grant this to us all! Amen.'

The theme of the sacrifice of ourselves was already present in the old liturgy, but it was drowned in the flood of words of a long prayer. Now it has been brought out into sharp relief as one of the essential moments of the Eucharistic service—as it is in the worship of the rest of Christendom. St Augustine, addressing some catechumens who were about to make their first Communion, affirmed the necessity of this sacrifice of ourselves in union with the unique sacrifice of Jesus Christ: 'You are there on the altar,' he said to them. 'You are there in the chalice.' Crucified with Christ, as St. Paul said. It is true that this offering of ourselves is never, and cannot ever be, any more than a response. But though the love and sacrifice of Christ constitute the call without which no response is possible, our response is nevertheless necessary, and without it there can be no true Holy Communion with the crucified and resurrected Lord: we should be left alone in our egoism.

But that is not all. It is not a case of my offering myself individually to Jesus Christ. I offer myself in and with the community. It is, then, the community, the Church itself which offers itself to God as a living and holy sacrifice, a sacrifice which is renewed at each celebration of the Lord's Supper, in communion with the sacrifice of Christ.

Thus our new liturgy, along with the meaning of Christian joy and victory, brings us also the meaning of sacrifice, and of the Church.

The prayer goes on: 'Thou who knowest the heart, purify us and renew in us the certain knowledge of thy pardon.' Thou who knowest the heart . . . we know our own hearts only imperfectly; usually we find easy excuses for ourselves; sometimes, on the other hand, we go to the opposite extreme, and become so downcast that we can scarcely believe forgiveness possible. But God knows us. 'If our heart condemn us, God is greater than our heart.' Rather than analysing ourselves and anxiously scrutinizing every corner of our conscience, let us dare to abandon ourselves to God who knows us, let us dare to rely on his forgiveness. Here again our liturgy comes back to the meaning of the Lord's Supper, which is not a reward for the righteous, but a pledge of forgiveness for sinners. There is then no question of our wondering if we are pure and holy enough to take part in the Communion. Are not the bread and wine there in order to testify to us by visible signs that God forgives? 'Here, then,' exclaims Calvin, 'is the peculiar consolation we receive from the Supper, that it directs and conducts us to the cross of Jesus Christ and to his resurrection, in order to assure us that, whatever iniquity there may be in us, the Lord does not cease to regard and accept us as righteous; whatever material of death may be in us, he does not cease to vivify us; whatever the wretchedness we may have, yet he does not cease to fill us with all felicity.'[1] The reformer is thinking of those poor consciences which would be troubled and thrown into a perilous perplexity if the Lord's Supper required one to bring to it 'an integrity of faith or life in which there was nothing with which to find fault'. With his robust good sense he concludes: 'If we allege as pretext for not coming to the Supper, that we are still weak in faith or in integrity of life, it is as if a man excuse himself from taking medicine because he is sick.'[2] To recognize oneself as a sinner, without pretending to rehearse the whole list of one's sins knowing 'how long a tail this monster of sin drags behind it, and that we never come to the end of it,' to repent and rely on God's forgiveness, is all that is required to approach the Holy Table with confidence. Jesus Christ did not come for the righteous.

The prayer continues: 'Send thy Holy Spirit upon us, that in receiving this bread and this cup, we may be partakers of the body and blood of our Lord Jesus Christ.' This is the *epiclesis* or invocation of the Holy Spirit. Note that the descent of the Holy Spirit is invoked not upon the bread and wine, but on the faithful, as living people. The bread and wine remain bread and wine, and have nothing to do with the divine action. The Holy Spirit acts upon persons and not upon things. The miracle, in the Holy

[1] Calvin, 'Treatise on the Holy Supper', in *Theological Treatises* (The Library of Christian Classics, Vol. XXII), SCM Press, London, 1954, p. 145.

[2] *Op. cit.*, p. 153.

Communion, is not that God transforms bread and wine, making them the substance of the body and blood of Christ, but that by the action of the Holy Ghost upon the faithful, they, eating the bread and drinking from the cup, are truly nourished by the flesh and blood of Christ, and partake in his life, becoming one with him through what one might call a blood-transfusion—a soul-transfusion.

The prayer concludes by taking up the prayer of the *Didache* or *Teaching of the Apostles*, a writing which probably dates from the end of the first century: 'As the ears once scattered in the fields and as the grapes once dispersed upon the hillsides are now gathered upon this table, in this bread and wine, so may thy whole Church, O Lord, soon be gathered in from the ends of the earth into thy Kingdom!' This intercession for the great ingathering of the Church into the Kingdom of God underlines the prophetic character of the Lord's Supper. The Eucharistic meal is, in fact, the anticipation and prefiguration of the great Messianic Feast to which Jesus was referring when, in the course of the Last Supper, he spoke of the fruit of the vine of which he would drink no more until the Kingdom of God should come (Luke 22.18). Here, then, is expressed the whole Christian hope—for unity at last realized, for the coming of God's Kingdom.

3. *The Biblical Foundations of the Eucharistic Liturgy*. The Liturgy of the Reformed Church of France, as I have briefly outlined it, seems to us to accord with the thought of St Paul, the apostle whose authority the Reformed Church loves to quote.

If we look at the account of the institution of the Lord's Supper as reported in the First Epistle to the Corinthians (I Cor. 11), and the commentary that accompanies it, we discover in the Lord's Supper the following essential 'moments':—

(i) The thanksgiving, or Eucharist properly so-called: 'He took bread, and when he had given thanks . . .'

(ii) The *anamnesis*, that is to say the commemoration of the sacrifice of Christ: 'This do in remembrance of me.'

(iii) The eschatological expectation: 'Ye do show the Lord's death till he come.'

(iv) The examination of conscience: 'Let a man examine himself.'

These, and no other, are the different moments whose remembrance constitutes our present liturgy of the Lord's Supper. Let us look at each one separately.

(i) *The thanksgiving.* The whole Communion service is a thanksgiving. This is what makes its joy, for thanksgiving is a manifestation of joy. The thanksgiving is shown in particular in the Preface and the *Benedictus*, and that is why we have gone back to these ancient forms, which are part of the liturgical heritage of the whole Church, remembering that Christianity did not begin with the Reformation in the sixteenth century.

(ii) *The anamnesis.* In our liturgy it is as follows: 'Holy and righteous Father, commemorating here the unique and perfect sacrifice offered once and for all on the cross by our Lord Jesus Christ. . . .' We are obeying here the Master's command: 'This do, in remembrance of me.' So every celebration of the Lord's Supper points to the Cross and commemorates the sacrifice of Calvary. The sacrifice is, as it were, made visible to us by the sight of the broken bread and the blood-red wine. For us, as for the Galatians (Gal. 3.1), the crucified Christ is depicted vividly. It is more than just a memorial—the memory, that is, of a past event. The Lord's Supper is a re-presentation of the event. It actualizes it; it makes it something that is happening now, so that its effects may be made operative, now and always. It is not just the memory of the upper room: the words and actions of Christ and of his disciples as they received the bread and the wine become once more present and alive. It is the same voice—his Voice—which invites us; it is the same hand—his Hand—which holds out to us the bread of life; it is the same love, the love that led him to the Cross, with which he loves us still.

(iii) *The eschatological expectation.* This was the very atmosphere of the Eucharist rather than a particular moment in its celebration.

The Supper was a foretaste and at the same time a prophecy of the great Messianic Feast. The prophetic significance of the Eucharist is often lost sight of. I have mentioned how by the insertion in our Liturgy of a fragment of prayer from the *Didache* we tried to make our celebration a great forward-looking act of hope, looking towards God's triumph over all the powers of evil.

(iv) *The examination of conscience.* This takes place in prayer and before God. 'Thou who knowest the heart . . .' It is taken up again in the thrice-repeated 'I am not worthy', which immediately precedes the communion. Paul insisted on this examination in view of the lack of seriousness which the Lord's Supper was celebrated at Corinth. It is known that it took place in the course of a church meal, the *agape*, and that the Corinthians had made it an orgy, some eating and drinking more than was reasonable, while others went hungry, thus showing an absence of brotherly charity which St Paul condemned. One can understand the apostle's exhortations to self-examination and his severity towards those who communicated not discerning the Lord's body and blood.

St Paul's words have given rise to many a scruple, and the little books of preparation for Communion which our grandparents used included a long and detailed examination of conscience, with the result that it was often only in a state of trembling trepidation that they approached the Holy Table. Such a religion, deeply serious, but also anxious and fearful as it was, seems to us today rather too gloomy. Of course the examination of conscience is necessary, and the Liturgy retains it as one of the chief elements in the service of the Lord's Supper; but one must not dwell too much upon this examination of oneself; one must not always be looking at oneself, as if looking in a mirror to detect the tiniest freckle on one's face, trying to uncover the slightest trace of dust in some corner of the soul. That is a self-regarding attitude, which concentrates on one's own good or bad qualities, one's own progress or backsliding, the purity or the blemishes of one's own character. It is egocentric and unhealthy, even though it may be the outcome of a desire for perfection. The true road to

45

sanctification is not found through endlessly cataloguing one's sins —even if it be in order to burn them like a sheaf of tares—but in looking towards Jesus Christ, in receiving him with all the more humility and thankfulness because we are sinners, in letting him live and grow in us. The opposite of sin, it has been remarked, is not virtue, but faith. And faith is communion with Jesus Christ. 'That he may dwell in us, and we in him.' It is for these reasons that the examination of conscience holds only a subordinate place in our Liturgy, and that it is made before God: 'Thou who knowest the heart. . . .'

The reader will see that our Liturgy does not set out to be innovatory. It remains closely linked to the teaching of St Paul, being based on the New Testament, whose lines it merely follows and prolongs. It seems to us to be truly evangelical. At the same time it breaks away from the individualism and the somewhat sombre character of the Reformed liturgies.

III. THE RESTORATION OF THE ECCLESIASTICAL YEAR

One of the innovations of the new Reformed Liturgy is the attention it gives to the ecclesiastical year. The old liturgy did indeed provide a few readings and prayers for the great Christian festivals, but it stopped there, taking no notice of the Sundays in Advent and Lent, or of those in the period between Easter and Whitsunday. Even so it was not in conformity with the Reformed tradition.

In Calvin's view all Sundays were identical, so that in *La forme des prières et chants ecclésiastiques* (Geneva, 1542) we find only the Sunday services, without any special forms for use at Christmas, Easter, or Whitsunday. As for the canticles, how could they have been adapted to the great feasts when, out of devotion to Holy Scripture, only the psalms were sung? So little attention was paid to what we call the Church's year that in the old registers in Geneva there is preserved an ordinance in which the Magistracy reminds pastors that it is their duty, during the week preceding the festival of Easter, to explain to the people the narratives of the Passion. That such an ordinance was necessary shows us to what an extent the observance of Holy Week itself was neglected.

It is true that in the preamble to the Liturgy of 1542 Calvin says, 'On working days the minister makes such exhortation to prayer as seems to him good, accommodating it to the time and to the matter of which he is treating in his preaching.' But the time to which Calvin here alludes is not that of the ecclesiastical year, but a time of plague or epidemic, or of war, drought, or public calamity generally. 'For this cause,' he says, 'if sometimes we see that God threatens us, it is good to have some day on which one may make prayers and supplications according to the exigencies of the time.'

In refusing to make any distinction between one Sunday and another, the Reformers thought to remain faithful to the words of St Paul, where he reproaches the Galatians for returning to bondage after having been called to liberty: 'Ye observe days, and months, and times, and years' (Gal. 4.10). They took these words literally, whereas in St Paul's mind they referred simply to a falling back into the Judaic law, and thence into paganism itself (legalistic observation of the Sabbath, new moons, the sabbatical year, etc.). What the apostle was condemning was the legalistic observation of such feasts, their obligatory and merit-earning character. 'When we, in the present age,' Calvin said, 'make a distinction of days, we do not represent them as necessary, and thus lay a snare for the conscience. . . . We do not make days to be the same thing with religion and the worship of God.'[1] The Reformers, then, did observe days, even though it was only by setting apart Sunday— and St Paul himself enjoins upon the Corinthians the observance of Easter (I Cor. 5.8).

It was only gradually, by a sort of internal necessity, and under the pressure of the piety of Christian people, that the

---

[1] *Commentaries on the Epistle to the Galatians*, translated by W. Pringle, Calvin Translation Society, Edinburgh, 1854, p. 124.

Reformed Churches of France came to adopt special prayers for the great festivals. The Ostervald Liturgy (1713) was the first to do so. In France, the first prayers for Christmas, New Year's Day, Palm Sunday, Good Friday, Easter Day, Ascensiontide and Whitsunday are to be found in a little liturgical collection entitled *Prières pour les Familles des Fidèles privées de l'Exercice public de leur Religion* ('Prayers for the Families of the Faithful deprived of the Public Exercise of their Religion') (2nd edition, 1758). It was, then, in private and family devotions that the observance of the ecclesiastical year first took root among us. In the Geneva Liturgy, which became after the Desert period the Liturgy of the Reformed Churches of France, it was only in 1724 that prayers were introduced for Christmas and the New Year, and more than a century later, in 1828, a solemn prayer for use on Good Friday. Not until 1868 do we find prayers for Easter and Whitsuntide. The French Liturgy of 1896 continued along the same road. Bersier, in his *Projet de révision de la liturgie des Eglises réformées de France*, wrote: 'The restoration of Christian worship in our churches requires firstly the re-establishment of the ecclesiastical year whose great seasons, from Christmas to Whitsuntide, recall the whole Christian drama. We have seen that these seasons were, so to speak, blotted out in the Reformed worship of the sixteenth century, and that they have been gradually regaining their place. Today the Church's year does in fact exist among us, and in this respect we are in communion with all the other Christian Churches. But it is necessary to give to this fact a more complete expression by creating an annual liturgical order to which the readings from Scripture and the songs of the people will be related.'

What the Liturgy of 1896 initiated under Bersier's inspiration, and what W. Monod outlined in the 'Watchers' Prayer-Book', our present liturgy continues and realizes in a completer fashion. Thus there are different words of adoration for each Sunday in the year, and special prayers and readings for Christmas, the Sundays of Lent, Holy Week, Easter, Ascension, and Whitsuntide. The period from Easter to Whitsunday is marked by a special 'salutation' recalling the fact that the Lord is risen. Lastly, for the service of the Lord's Supper there are different Prefaces related to the great events recalled by each of the festivals. Furthermore, in some churches the colour of the marker-ribbon in the altar Bible, or of the pulpit-fall, varies according to the Proper of the season.

Thus from Sunday to Sunday the mind of the Christian is led through the whole history of salvation, from the dark centuries of waiting which find their fulfilment in Christmas Day, up to the calling to mind of the last things and the time of the end of the world. It has been aptly said: 'Just as in the order of nature the old terrestrial creation makes in one year the journey round the physical sun, so in the order of grace the Church, the first-fruits of the new creation, turns in one year about its spiritual sun, Christ, so as to receive all its rays, and to contemplate its varied aspects.'[1]

IV. THE DECALOGUE AND ITS PLACE IN WORSHIP

Characteristic of Reformed worship is its liturgical use of the Ten Commandments. In the little church used by the French refugees in Strasbourg, when Calvin was its pastor, they were read —or, to be more exact, they were sung—after the confession and absolution. The liturgical use of the Decalogue goes back to the very earliest forms of worship of the Reformation in France. It was already included in Farel's 1536 Liturgy, *La manière et fasson*.

The origin of this liturgical use of the Decalogue is still a matter of conjecture. But what is important is not so much the use itself, as the place it takes in the order of service. Originally it was said or sung after the absolution. Now it is read at the very beginning of the service, immediately after the invocation.

The place of the Ten Commandments in the *Ordo* is not a matter of indifference. It has a theological importance which ought to be made clear.

[1] R. Paquier, *op. cit.*, p. 94.

The Reformers distinguished three 'uses' of the Law:

1. The *usus civilis*. The Law acts as a bridle on men's passions enabling them to live together without tearing one another to pieces. This might be called the sociological use.

2. The *usus paedagogicus*. The Law leads us to Christ through the sense of sin that it awakens in us when we consider our failings.

3. The *usus normativus*. The Law is the norm of the Christian life. The believer must observe God's commandments.

Luther stressed the pedagogical use. The Law leads to repentance and forgiveness. He saw in it the history of his own life, the road of ordinances and works having led him, through despair, to the revelation of the grace which is in Jesus Christ. The placing of the Decalogue at the beginning of the service and before the confession underlines this pedagogical use of the Law.

Calvin, for his part, without rejecting the other two uses, stresses principally the normative use of the Law. The law shows the road upon which the regenerate Christian does in fact walk, in spite of his frequent stumblings. It is addressed not to the impenitent sinner in order to bring him to a recognition of his sin and to repentance, but to the forgiven child in order to mark out the road his faithfulness must follow; hence its place after the absolution.

Thus, while the pedagogical use of the Law emphasizes our incapacity to keep it, and puts it before us in order to reproach us for having broken it, the normative use, on the other hand, shows us obedience to the Law as something possible with God's help, and something, moreover, which is normal, in spite of the failings of the very saints themselves. It was in order to emphasize this normative use of the Law that Calvin, at Strasbourg, put it after the absolution. The aim of the Law was not to bring us to repentance, but to convey to us, as it were, the orders of the leader to his troops, the rule of life which the Father requires of his children now pardoned.

Today the Decalogue is read before the confession of sin and the promises of forgiveness. Who is responsible for this displacement of the Decalogue which accentuates in our worship the Lutheran use of the Law?

It is to be noted that when Calvin returned to Geneva in 1541 the Decalogue seems to have disappeared from the Liturgy. It is true that in an appendix, together with several psalms and the *Nunc dimittis*, there appears a metrical version of the Decalogue, or rather a somewhat free adaptation of it. This rhymed—I hesitate to call it poetic—version of the Law, interrupted at regular intervals by a *Kyrie eleison*, could thus on occasion be sung, but there is no evidence that it was sung regularly. In any case, while Calvin was still alive, a new metrical version of the Decalogue was published—this time by Clément Marot: 'Raise the heart, open the ear. . . .' This version replaced the preceding one—a substitution which would be unthinkable in the case of a traditional liturgical text used regularly in worship.

In fact it was long after Calvin's day, in the seventeenth century (in 1639, to be exact), that the Ten Commandments were introduced into worship in Geneva. In the registers of the Venerable Company of Pastors, against the date of Friday, 9th August, 1639, we read that on the previous day it had been resolved in consistory that on Sundays the Commandments of God should be read from the pulpit. This was to be done at the beginning of the service, for two reasons, firstly in order to engage the attention of the congregation, and secondly because it was more convenient for the pastor. The old register goes on to give these precise instructions: 'This reading will be done by the usual readers, and this as the last stroke of the bell is sounded.' The Decalogue therefore at Geneva acted as a sort of preface or introduction to the service proper. It was read even before the service had really begun, by a theological student, in order to cover up the noise of late arrivals and the shuffling of chairs. Later it was integrated into the service itself, but remained at the very beginning, before the confession. The Liturgical Commission of the Reformed Church of France proposed a return to the authentic Reformation tradition, putting the Law back in its old place after the Confession. But this recommendation was not accepted by the Synods, which thought it would not be possible to upset a habit of such long standing.

V. THEOLOGICAL FACTORS IN THE LITURGICAL REVIVAL

The liturgical movement in the Reformed Churches is not an autonomous one; it is related to other movements and is linked with other revivals, of which it is a consequence and which in turn it amplifies.

1. It is first of all the sign of a new consciousness of the Church as such. The Reformed Protestant, as perhaps any Protestant must be, is by training profoundly individualistic; and, as I have said, individualism is the sworn enemy of all liturgy. Like fire and water, they do not mix. The very essence of a liturgy is that it is common prayer. Like the Lord's Prayer, which is its pattern, liturgical prayer does not say 'I', but 'We'. That is to say that the voice which is heard in the liturgy is not the intimate and personal voice of the individual soul, but the voice of the Church; and not only the voice of the community temporarily formed by the congregation of believers in one place, but the voice of the universal Church, past as well as present, the voice of the great mystical body of Jesus Christ. Through the liturgy we make our own the repentance, the intercession, the confession of faith, and the hope of the whole Church. We take our place in the great company of the 'Communion of Saints'. 'The believer,' writes Guardini, 'if he is actively living the liturgical life, must be conscious that he is living and acting as a member of the Church, and that it in its turn is praying and acting in him.' In this way the liturgy takes us out of ourselves, it draws us out of our self-centred solitude, and quickens us by thrusting us back into the life of the community, and gathering us up into the great unity of the Body of Christ. It is necessary to have the

vision of this unity if we are to understand the meaning of the liturgy.

Now the Protestant, despite his deep-rooted individualism, is in process of rediscovering the meaning of the Church. This is the whole trend of the theology of recent decades. Increasing numbers of books have been published, studying and defining the doctrine of the Body of Christ. Half a century ago it was scarcely ever mentioned, whereas today it is becoming of prime importance. The very word 'community' is on everyone's lips, and is witnessed to by deeds. The brothers of Taizé and the sisters of Pomeyrol in France, and in Switzerland the sisters of Grandchamp, live a community life, alternating the discipline of prayer with that of work, having all their goods in common and practising poverty, obedience, and celibacy, actually within the old Huguenot Protestantism. Only a very few years ago this return to a monastic form of life would have been absolutely unthinkable.

This new sense of the Church shows itself in a revival of participation in the Eucharist. I recall without joy the services of the Lord's Supper in the big Protestant town in which I spent my childhood. After the sermon there was a general exodus. There remained to take part in the Communion only a few aged women, almost all in mourning, and even fewer men. The atmosphere was funereal. Today our members are finding their way back to the Holy Table. Services of Holy Communion are more frequent; instead of four celebrations annually, the meagre heritage from Geneva, which had remained intact until the beginning of this century, the Lord's Supper is celebrated at least once a month. More and more are coming to it, and the proportion of young people is a joy to see, especially in urban churches.

It is understandable that such a revival of Eucharistic life should have called for a revision of the Eucharistic liturgy. In its turn, a Eucharistic liturgy that is less didactic, more lively and joyful, attracts young people to the Lord's Supper and teaches them to love it. Holy Communion is no longer an extraordinary and exceptional act, simply because of being so infrequent, an occasion for which one spent several days—and sometimes weeks —in preparation, examining one's conscience, and which one approached in fear and trembling. It is becoming a normal act of Christian life, just as normal as eating and drinking are for the life of the body.

A second sign of the rediscovery of the meaning of the Church seems to me to be the place accorded to intercession. Intercession is a duty which proceeds from the reality of the Church. In fact we are all, as Christians, bound one to another, and all to Christ, and through him to God. We are parts of a living organism; we are responsible for all those who with us are members of the same body, members of Christ. It follows that the life of the Christian cannot be isolated, self-centred, separated by impassable barriers from the lives of others. His life, in so far as it is truly Christian, is part of the life of the whole body, and is dependent on that common life. One life unites all the members that go to make up the body, just as in the vine the same sap permeates all the shoots.

In virtue of this unity, which makes the Church one body in Christ, there is communication between the various cells of the body. 'Whether one member suffer, all the members suffer with it,' asserts St Paul. On the other hand, when a Christian intercedes for his brethren, there takes place as it were a regeneration of the devitalized cells of the organism. His faith and fervour go mysteriously, like the blood purified by the lungs, to restore the strength and vigour of faltering souls. The more so as it is not *his* faith and *his* fervour which go directly to quicken those for whom he prays, but Christ and the grace of Christ. Contact is established and the current of life restored only by prayer. It is thus the divine strength in all its power which uses, if one may put it so, the thin fragile wire that intercessory prayer, inspired by love, stretches for a moment between men's souls.

These are only analogies taken from the world of things. They are doubtless always inadequate in some respects, and one must not press them too far. They may nevertheless throw some light on the quite spiritual interdependence of souls in Christ. It is comprehensible that the return to an understanding of the Church as the Body of Christ, stressing as it does the interdependence of all Christians in him, should have encouraged the practice of intercessory prayer.

It is in fact practised regularly by the Taizé, Pomeyrol, and Grandchamp communities, which see it as one of their essential tasks, as it is also their aim to recall us all to the great duty of intercession.

The new Liturgy, also, accords to intercession a much greater place than in the past. There are prayers for the Church— its reawakening, its witness, its unity—for the vocations which the Church needs, for theological faculties, for the councils of the Church, for the Churches of the whole world, and especially the Roman Church, and for those who have to suffer for Christ's sake. There are prayers for missions, for the Jews and for Islam; for evangelistic work, for young people, for Sunday Schools, and for young men under arms. There are prayers for workers, both in agriculture and in industry, for both employers and employees, for scientists, artists, and journalists. There are prayers for the sick and infirm, for the aged and the afflicted, for travellers, and so on. No liturgy has ever contained such an abundant wealth of forms of prayer to help the faithful in their intercessions.

Thus the new awareness of the meaning of the Church, manifesting itself in a 'revitalization' of Eucharistic life and of intercessory prayer, shows itself incontestably to be one of the factors in the liturgical movement; and the liturgical movement in its turn reinforces this awareness of the meaning of the Church.

2. A second determining factor of the liturgical revival is without doubt the dogmatic revival which is taking place in our time. The end of the nineteenth century and the beginning of the twentieth was marked by fideism on the one hand, and counterbalancing it on the other, a rigid orthodoxy which was more often repeated like a slogan than carefully thought out. Now the accent is being put on doctrine. It is seen as the source of the whole life of the Church. Even preaching is becoming doctrinal. It is

possible to see the influence of Karl Barth in this dogmatic revival, but he is not its sole initiator. There has been developing concurrently a new Calvinism which reasserts the great doctrinal affirmations of the French reformer. This revival is witnessed to by the popularity of reviews such as *La Revue réformée*, published by the Calvinist Society of France, *Verbum Caro* in Switzerland, and especially *Les Cahiers de l'actualité protestante*, published by Delachaux and Niestlé. At the same time the *Institutio Christianae Religionis*, the source-book of Reformed dogma, has been republished in two editions, one in popular form for the general reader, and the other a critical edition for the scholar, reproducing the text of 1560, the last to which Calvin himself put his hand, and recording all the variant readings of the earlier editions.

This doctrinal revival is without doubt one of the factors in the liturgical revival. The Liturgy, indeed, moves in the serene and majestic domain of the great dogmatic affirmations. It is, as has been said, prayer woven with dogma. Sunday by Sunday it proclaims the great basic truths of Christianity: the holiness of God, the judgement of sinful man, redemption in Jesus Christ, salvation by faith. And if to the forms of Sunday worship are added those for Baptism and Holy Communion, one finds that in this service-book one has the Gospel—in brief, of course, but nevertheless the whole Gospel.

We all tend to see only one limited aspect of the truth of the Gospel. We are dazzled by one particular colour of the spectrum, and see that colour only. The liturgy, however, reaffirms and maintains the great verities of our faith in their organic relationship, helping us to see the whole. It does not, of course, pretend to say everything that there is to be said. Like the Catechism it is a summary, but—like the Catechism—it aims to say what must be said, to pray what must be prayed, and to proclaim, as the Catechism does, the essential truths of the Christian faith. As Bossuet asserted, 'the principal instrument of the Church's tradition is contained in its prayers'.

Further, the doctrinal revival has pushed into the background the sentimental effusions of pietism, and emotionalism in general, stressing the importance of thought, which alone has universal value, and which alone is always faithful to itself. In this it accords with the nature of liturgical worship, which imposes on itself and on us the greatest reserve. It is a stranger to the expression of excessive sentiment, to the radical resolutions which can turn a person's life upside down, like the convulsive repentance of the sinner on the bench of the confessional. It shows a certain modesty, avoiding the display of the soul's secrets. It prefers to leave discreetly in the shadow what passes between the soul and God, throwing over this mystery the veil of its imagery and solemnity. It turns its back on expansive self-expression and spiritual prattle. Liturgical worship may for this reason seem to some to be dry and cold, and pietistic circles are usually averse to it. There is, however, a deep concordance between dogma and liturgy, between the doctrinal bias of our time and the 'truth clothed in prayer' which is what liturgical worship is.

The dogmatic revival has also brought into the foreground the Person and work of Christ, and here again there is seen to be a close concordance between the doctrine of the Church and its liturgy. Christ fills the liturgy altogether; he is its centre. It is through Jesus Christ our Lord that the Church speaks to God. The greater the fervour for Christ, the more living the liturgy becomes.

This Christocentric doctrinal position goes to explain, in part at least, the intensification of sacramental life which we have noted in the Reformed Church of France, and its new interest in liturgical worship. For Christ is present in the Holy Communion; it is our communion with him which takes place there; it is our privilege to sup with him at his table; there we receive remission of our sins by his blood. The Last Supper in the upper room is not merely re-enacted as in a sort of *tableau vivant*—it is lived as a present reality; it is not a memorial only that we celebrate: the joy of the Holy Communion is that Christ is there.

In the same way the baptismal liturgy is centred wholly upon

Christ. We are buried by Baptism in his death, at once to rise again with him. It is then, with his death, Christ's resurrection which is evoked as the image of the new life which is henceforth that of the baptized person. In fact the rite of Baptism reproduces liturgically the whole Christian drama: the death and resurrection of Christ. The symbolism is different from that of the Eucharist, but they refer to the same reality. The great redeeming drama of salvation is set before our eyes. All the liturgists see in the water of Baptism, as in the wine of the Lord's Supper, the blood of Jesus Christ. 'Baptism,' says Calvin, 'promises us no other purification than by the sprinkling of the blood of Christ; which is emblematically represented by water, on account of its resemblance to washing and cleansing.'[1]

Properly understood, this means that Baptism symbolically reproduces before our eyes the redemptive drama of Calvary.

Apart from Jesus Christ the Sacraments of the Church are meaningless. They become a reality in so far as faith in Christ is itself a reality. Their purpose is 'to fasten us fully upon Christ'. They are like mirrors in which we may see him and contemplate his work of redemption.

The Christocentric doctrinal attitude shows itself again in the liturgy in the introduction of the ecclesiastical year, of which we have spoken.

Thus in various ways the doctrinal revival has been a factor in the liturgical revival, giving new life to the great affirmations of the symbols of faith, and returning to the Sacraments their pre-eminence in the life of the believer. On the other hand, the Christocentric nature of the liturgy has been reinforcing the Christocentric dogmatic position, making it more than a doctrinal position—incorporating it concretely into the life of the Church.

3. A third factor in the liturgical revival has certainly been the concentration of theological thought on worship. Public worship

---

[1] *Institutio Christianae religionis*, IV. xv. 2 (English version: *The Institutes of the Christian Religion*, translated by John Allen, James Clarke & Co., London, 1935, Vol. II, p. 478).

is one of the burning questions of the day. The result has been a heightened interest in liturgical matters, and this interest has in its turn had the effect of calling the attention of all believers to the question of worship. Since the first world war there has been a steady stream of books, pamphlets and articles concerning worship, among them the monumental work in three volumes by my colleague Professor R. Will.[1]

There is not room here even for a brief sketch of the theology of worship. It must suffice to point out how worship is at once a dialogue and an act of praise.

(i) *A dialogue.* This is the definition that Luther himself gave of it in his sermon at the dedication of the chapel of Torgau. 'The event which we call worship,' he said, 'consists simply in this, that our well-beloved Lord himself speaks to us by his Holy Word, and we, for our part, speak to him by our prayers and our hymns of praise.'

It is characteristic of this dialogue that it is not the dialogue of the individual alone face to face with his God, but of the whole community with the God who has manifested himself as the Father of all—our Father.

This dialogue is communion. Behind the words of the dialogue there are living realities. God's Word is not mere discursive intellectual explanation intended to enlighten our minds; it is an act of God, a creative word, a sovereign *Fiat*. It is a word which breaks, which overthrows, which lays hold on man and calls into being that which does not exist. God's Word is inseparable from his grace; for the soul which hears it, it is the gift of grace. In its full sense, the Word of God is God himself communicating himself and giving himself to us.

Man's reply to God is also a living word, a word that expresses realities, a word which is a giving of ourselves, so that the dialogue of worship becomes an effective encounter by the community with God, the community offering itself to God in its weakness and

[1] R. Will, *Le Culte*, Faculté de Théologie protestante de l'Université de Strasbourg, 1925-35.

nakedness, and God coming to the community in self-giving power.

(ii) *An act of praise.* It is true that the assembled community receives from God strength, consolation and hope. But it is there essentially to worship him, to praise and adore him. 'The liturgy,' the encyclical *Mediator Dei* said, 'is the integral worship of the mystical body.' The God-centred character of worship is thus underlined. Worship is less for man, to fulfil his aspirations and needs, than for God.

From these theoretical considerations concerning worship there have flowed, as regards the Liturgy, three consequences.

Firstly the greater place accorded to silent worship. This may appear paradoxical. If worship is dialogue, does it not require that there shall be continual discourse? That was how our fathers understood it. For centuries, in their care to stress the catechetical and didactic character of worship, they made it the explanation of a written word rather than the transmission of a living word. They thus laid themselves open to the criticism of Vinet, who complained that our worship was too intellectual, having everything made articulate, everything spoken. But a profounder understanding of the dialogue has led to a realization that silence is still a form of the dialogue of worship: even, perhaps, one of its culminating points. God does indeed speak in the silence; it is then perhaps that one hears his voice most clearly; it is then that he can apply to each individually the word which is addressed to all in the sermon. And we can speak to God in the silence. We can make it the moment of our personal response, of our dedication of ourselves to the service that awaits us. We are thinking of course of the inner silence of the soul, which shuts its ears to the solicitations and distractions of the world, turning wholly towards God in the receptive attitude of prayer, a silence which bears in itself, in some measure, its own fulfilment. But external silence can assist this inner silence. It can be a preparation for it and at the same time a manifestation of it. How moving this silence can be —charged with prayer, thrilling with the presence of God!

It is necessary to rid ourselves of the tenacious idea that prayer must always be expressed in words and formulae. The truth is that there are some silences that are richer, truer, more telling than words, and which are sincerer prayers than any formal prayers could be: silences of humility, silences of acceptance, silences of adoration, silences of intercession. It is written: 'Keep silence before the Lord,' and that is also a form of prayer. May we not give our whole heart in silence? Someone has remarked that 'words fail us more often when we pray than at any other time'.

In spite of ingrained habits the new Reformed Liturgy attempts to acclimatize silence in our traditional worship and forms of service. It refrains from watering it down, for instance, by drowning it in a voluntary on the organ, which would be to destroy it altogether. The new rubric allows for a short silence after the preaching of the Word, which may be followed by a brief organ voluntary. Several times besides, the Liturgy introduces silence into the worship by intercalating between the sentences of certain prayers the word 'Pause', to indicate a period of silence. In the Eucharist, after the Preface and after the Communion, there is provision for silence—a silence which is a form of prayer and adoration.

Adoration is one of the essential functions of worship which the new Liturgy attempts to make more living. It flows from the God-centred character of worship. Worship of God must be adoration since God is God. Man's normal attitude, as soon as he is aware of the presence of God, is adoration. It follows that the whole of worship must be adoration; adoration is as it were its atmosphere, the perfume that arises from it and fills the whole house, like the odour of the ointment with which Mary anointed Christ's feet at Bethany.

There is no adoration without humility. In the presence of the Lord man feels his littleness, his nothingness. He is as it were prostrated before the divine majesty. He says with Abraham: 'Behold now, I have taken upon me to speak unto the Lord, which am but dust and ashes' (Gen. 18.27). The greatness of God his

Creator is branded on man's mind; and it is the lively realization
of God's glory which reminds him of the true hierarchies: God
first—'*Sire Dieu premier servi!*' (God the King served first!).
This drawing back in fear is accentuated when in God's presence
we realize not only our smallness but also our sin. God is not
only almighty, but also all holy—the thrice-holy God. With Isaiah
who saw in the temple that divine holiness, we cry: 'Woe is me!
for I am undone.' We would flee: 'Depart from me; for I am a
sinful man, O Lord.'

But alongside this desire to escape there is in adoration a
movement towards God. Our faith and our love impel us towards
him when we see him in Jesus Christ, and when we accept his
forgiveness and his grace. Adoration is thus a kind of equilibrium
between fear and joy, a stillness in which the whole attention of the
worshipper is concentrated on God. All worship must be offered
in this atmosphere of adoration; it is adoration which gives it
warmth and life; it is this communion in adoration which ought
to take hold, irresistibly, of all who venture into the holy place,
making them aware, in some measure, of the very presence of
God.

Nevertheless there is a place in the dialogue of worship for
those special moments when adoration becomes more explicit.
The new Liturgy seeks to introduce such moments. At the beginning of the form of service for Sunday there appears the rubric,
'Adoration'. There follow several texts, chosen mainly from the
Psalter, by means of which the congregation utters God's praise
and exalts his glory, as does also the singing of the psalm which
follows. Thus every Sunday worship begins with this moment of
adoration. Elsewhere adoration takes the form of a mystic dialogue
between Christ and the Christian, as, for example, in the form of
worship for Christmas Eve. As these dialogues are a new departure
in our liturgies I give an example here:

℣. I am the light of the world: he that followeth me shall not walk
  in darkness, but shall have the light of life.

℟. Lighten us, O Lord, and teach us to walk as children of light.

℣. I am the way. No man cometh unto the Father, but by me.

℟. Lord, lead us into the arms of the Father.

℣. I am the truth and the life.

℟. Lord, deliver us from error. Grant us to live in thee, and do thou come and live in us.

℣. I am the good shepherd: the good shepherd giveth his life for the sheep.

℟. Lord, make me one of the sheep of thy hand.

℣. I am the door of the sheep: by me if any man enter in, he shall be saved.

℟. Lord, open to us the door of thy sheepfold.

℣. I am the bread of life: he that cometh unto me shall never hunger; and he that believeth on me shall never thirst.

℟. Lord, fill our hungry souls and water our thirsty hearts.

℣. I am the vine, ye are the branches: he that abideth in me, and I in him, the same bringeth forth much fruit.

℟. Lord, give us grace to bring forth fruit to thy glory.

℣. I am the bright and morning star.

℟. Lord, who announcest eternal day, come quickly.

And so on.

Adoration disposes the heart to contemplation. Our contemplation is directed less towards the invisible God than to Jesus Christ who has revealed him to us, and who in his humanity became one of us. The Liturgy in several places thus invites us to contemplation, especially in the services for Holy Week, and in the Lord's Supper. There is also a 'contemplation' in the funeral service for a child:

'Grant to us to contemplate thee, thou shepherd of heaven, holding to thy heart the child whom we commend to thee. With thy whole flock thou leadest him unto living fountains of waters. Thou hast already wiped away all tears from his eyes.'

63

As the reader will see, the new Liturgy attempts to rectify the aridity which has often been complained of in Reformed worship. It interrupts the unending flow of words with moments of silence, prolonging the spoken dialogue in a discreeter dialogue which can only be pursued in the secret places of the heart.

In accordance with the concept of worship revealed by recent studies, the Liturgy attempts also to accord a place to joy.

It gives a greater place to praise, using the singing of psalms. And to praise God is joy.

Thanksgiving is also a joy. It turns us away from our preoccupation with ourselves, our scruples, and even from our sense of sin, directing our gaze towards him in whom God gives us all things. It happens that though we are always ready to ask, we are not so quick to thank the Lord for his blessings. We pray: 'Deliver us from evil, forgive us, grant us . . .' But we fail to render thanks when we have been granted victories and deliverances. Here is a prayer of thanksgiving from the Liturgy:

'For the victories which thou hast given us to win over doubt and
    temptation,
For thy help and deliverance,
Our thankful hearts adore thee . . .'

I have already mentioned the introduction of the element of joy in the Eucharist, with the Preface and the *Benedictus*. The tragedy of the Cross must give a solemn and serious character to the Lord's Supper, but it must not banish joy from it altogether, for in the New Testament the Cross makes men sing for joy, for it is our salvation. It was thus that it was understood by the seer of the Revelation: 'Unto him that loveth us, and loosed us from our sins by his blood . . .; to him be the glory and the dominion for ever and ever.' St Paul exults in the face of the Cross, uttering a cry of joyful triumph which he cannot contain as he contemplates the vision of the crucified Christ: 'Who is he that shall condemn? It is Christ that died. . . .' Those historians who have thought to see two different kinds of Eucharist in the New Testament—that of joy and gladness, the Eucharist of the Resurrection, represented by the breaking of bread in Jerusalem, and the sombre, almost funereal Eucharist of the Pauline Supper —are singularly mistaken. The memory of death and the joy of thanksgiving are by no means irreconcilable. The primitive Supper could very well contain that note of joy and gladness to which these historians are pleased to point, although it also recalled the Lord's death: indeed, just because it recalled his death. It is only when faith becomes weak, and is replaced by a false sentimentality, that the theme of the Passion, instead of awakening grateful joy in the heart, becomes a funereal theme.

This is the spirit in which the new Liturgy concludes the Good Friday service by adoring him who is alive for evermore, and who hereafter holds the keys of death and of Hades.

It seems that we have found again the true meaning of worship, which is a joyful dialogue between the child and his Father, between the Church and her Lord, a dialogue which is communion, and which may sometimes be carried on in silence; such a dialogue as Adolphe Monod sang of:

> *Heureux quand je t'écoute, et que cette parole*
> *Qui dit: 'Lumière, sois;' et la lumière fut,*
> *S'abaisse jusqu'à moi, m'instruit et me console,*
> *Et me dit: 'C'est ici le chemin du salut.'*
>
> *Heureux quand je te parle, et que de ma poussière*
> *Je fais monter vers toi mon hommage et mon vœu,*
> *Avec la liberté d'un fils devant son père,*
> *Et le saint tremblement d'un pécheur devant Dieu.*[1]

[1] Happy am I when I listen to thee, and when that word
Which said: 'Let there be light!' and there was light,
Comes down even to me, to instruct and console me,
And says to me: 'Here lies the way of salvation.'

Happy am I when I speak to thee, and when from my dust
I raise to thee my homage and my prayer,
With the liberty of a son before his father,
And the holy trembling of a sinner before God.

It should be noted that while I have chiefly considered the new Liturgy of the Reformed Church of France, the same characteristics are to be found in other recent liturgies in French. The movement is general in most Churches, and is marked increasingly by a return to a more ecumenical outlook. It bears witness to a real revival of religious life, and also itself contributes to that revival.

VI. LITURGY AND TRADITION

The restorations and developments I have been describing have not been the work of scholars or aesthetes desirous of a return to ancient forms. The liturgist is not like an archaeologist in a museum of antiquities, trying to resurrect half-effaced texts from the dust of centuries, delighting in his discoveries. He is a man of today, thinking of his fellow-Christians, working for them, seeking to express their needs, their aspirations, their prayers and praises, as well as the undeviating faith of the Church.

In any case, one must set aside the idea that the primitive Church was the ideal Church, and that our whole aim ought to be simply to reproduce its original features. There were racial conflicts within it (Hellenists against Hebrews), there were bickerings, parties—that of Peter, that of Apollos, and that of Paul; there was that same cupidity which has shown itself in every century since (Ananias and Sapphira); there were dogmatic disputes, and violent personal clashes (I am thinking of the altercation—which must have been quite lively—between Peter and Paul at Antioch, and of the estrangement between Paul and Barnabas over Mark); there were serious moral scandals; there were cranks, *illuminati*, fanatics, separatists, bunglers, ambitious persons such as Diotrephes, who loved 'to have the pre-eminence among them' (III John 9). It is necessary then, in our thinking about the primitive Church, to rid ourselves of the notion of a Golden Age. The Church seems always to have been what it is today, with its saints, its faithful and its lukewarm adherents, and its hypocrites. This is something we ought as Christians to be humble about, but it is also an encouragement to us when we are worried by the state of our own parishes, to know from history and from the Gospel that God does not abandon his Church, but continues to work for it in spite of its shortcomings and its lack of faith.

The liturgy, then, cannot be simply a return to the past. It does not develop artificially and arbitrarily; it is a living, growing organism, a tree which develops and is always sending out new shoots. The liturgy is an uninterrupted stream, a living spring of prayer throughout the centuries, sustaining the prayer of the Church and our own individual prayers. To this great river of liturgical life, which is one with the stream of Christian life itself, we must continually be returning, so that our liturgies do not become little streams at its margins which soon lose themselves in sterile backwaters.

The stream can be enriched as the years pass. To deny that the centuries have brought their tribute of pure spring waters to swell the river of Christian liturgy, would be to deny the presence and the action of the Holy Spirit in the Church. The liturgy is not a closed tradition, turned in upon itself. It is, in the Bergsonian sense, an open tradition.

But to call it an open tradition is to accept the possibility of parasitic developments—even of actual divergences. I am thinking in particular of Marian devotions and of the litanies of the saints. It is therefore necessary to have a constant control of liturgy by Scripture. The liturgy must not deviate from Scripture. In fact, the valid liturgical developments are those which spring spontaneously from the piety of the Church, enlivened by Scripture and in its fidelity to Scripture. Finally, the deciding factor is Christian judgement—the Church, not necessarily in its hierarchy, but in its experience and its living continuity. In doing so the Church uses a certain spiritual tact, a certain discernment, a certain evangelical sensitivity. There are some liturgical texts and experiments which the consensus of believers accepts, and others which it rejects.

In so doing it acts naturally, organically, without needing a council or an ecclesiastical decision. It is in this living conscience of the Church, and more especially in its worship, that we must seek the continuity of its tradition. The more the Church is nourished on the Bible, the more surely and spontaneously does it effect this process of assimilation and elimination, by which its true tradition is formed.

For my part I gladly greet the advent of the new Liturgy of the Reformed Church of France. It marks a break with old errors. It brings us back from a position that was too isolated, setting us once again in the mainstream of Christian Eucharistic tradition. It brings us closer to the other Churches, but without compromising, abandoning or distorting our Evangelical principles. Under God and through the action of the Holy Spirit, this may be an event big with promise for the future.

RECENT LITURGICAL DEVELOPMENTS IN THE ROMAN CATHOLIC CHURCH

THE religious movement of our time is characterized by an undoubted revival both dogmatic and liturgical. This is as true of Roman Catholicism as it is of Protestantism.

Although dogma and liturgy are intimately connected—*lex orandi lex credendi*—we shall be considering here only the liturgical movement in contemporary Roman Catholicism, more especially in France.

I. A BRIEF HISTORICAL SURVEY

There is no room here to trace in detail the history of the movement; all that is possible is to give a brief sketch.

Following the decisions of Pope Pius V, reorganizing the liturgy of the Roman Church on the basis of the resolutions of the Council of Trent, and unifying the innumerable forms and rubrics which had reduced the liturgy to a confusing and unwieldy conglomeration, a petrification had taken place. It is not until the beginning of the twentieth century that we see signs of what one might call the liturgical thaw. Even then this thaw did not come as a matter of course; it met at first with no little indifference.

Mgr Wagner records that when in 1909 Catholics assembled in Belgium for the Congress of Malines, Cardinal Mercier wished to give an opportunity to speak in one of the sessions of the Congress to a young Benedictine from Mont César in Louvain, who had previously convinced him that the faith of the Church was to be learnt in its liturgy, and that consequently it was of especial importance that church members should understand and take part in it.

No one wanted to accept this report, but out of deference to the wishes of the Cardinal it was eventually found a place in the

Christian Art and Archaeology section. Thus it was under the aegis of Christian art that Dom Lambert Beaudouin delivered his epoch-making speech foreshadowing the liturgical movement.[1]

In his opening address to the Congress of Assisi, in September 1956, Cardinal Cicognani did homage to the venerable memory of Dom Lambert Beaudouin, declaring that he could be considered as the father of the modern liturgical movement.[2]

Along with that of Dom Beaudouin, one should also quote the names of Dom Ildefons Herwegen, parish priest of Maria-Laach, and of Dom Odo Cassel, who died recently, both of whom were among the prime movers of the present liturgical revival.

Evidence of this revival is the creation in France of the 'Centre de Pastorale Liturgique', whose organ is the review *La Maison-Dieu*. The association in the name of this organization of the two terms 'liturgical' and 'pastoral' is a good indication of the general tenor of the movement. The primary intention is not erudite research, but the consideration of the needs of church members, and the encouragement of their effective participation in the liturgical life of the Church.

'What is new in this generation compared with the preceding one,' says Fr Doncoeur, 'is the way in which interest in the liturgy is no longer confined to specialist scholars, but has become the serious preoccupation of an ever-widening circle of the most active members of the clergy, and that even further, lay people generally have begun to take part in a profound revival of liturgical life.'[3]

Spontaneous developments of various kinds nearly everywhere have borne witness to the creative exuberance of the movement, and provoked in 1947 the encyclical of Pius XII, *Mediator Dei et hominum*. This, like most encyclicals, does not inaugurate a new movement in the Church; rather does it bear witness to the reality and vitality of a movement already in existence. It does not create it: it sanctions it and at the same time controls, harmonizes

[1] *La Maison-Dieu*, Nos. 47-8, 1956, IV, p. 107.   [2] *Ibid.*, p. 27.
[3] *La Maison-Dieu*, No. 25, 1951, I, p. 5.

and limits it. It is like the secateurs with which the good gardener prunes the new growth, cutting out suckers, and maintains the good order of the whole plant by removing growths that would spoil it. Fr Doncoeur describes this encyclical, somewhat exaggeratedly perhaps, as 'unprecedented among the acts of the *magisterium* of the Church'; Cardinal Cicognani calls it the 'great charter of the liturgy', echoing the words of Dom Beaudouin: 'the solemn charter of the liturgy'. However one looks at it, it is an important pronouncement by the Hierarchy, since it sets out to define the liturgy and its part in the life of the Church.

After the Papal Encyclical came the *General Decretal for the Simplification of the Rubrics*, published in 1955 by the Sacred Congregation of Rites, and finally the Decretal *Maxima redemptionis nostrae mysteria*, of the 16th November, 1955, instituting a new *Ordo* for Holy Week. We shall study first the liturgical movement as a whole, its underlying tendencies, the needs to which it aims to respond, and the opposition it is meeting. Thereafter we shall examine more briefly what has come to be called the restoration of Holy Week. I shall conclude with a few general remarks.

II. DEVELOPMENTS IN THE LITURGY OF THE MASS

1. *Participation by the People in the Mass*

The point of departure of the liturgical movement was, so to speak, a negative one. It was the painful and almost universal realization that the priest was saying the Mass to some extent in a void, the congregation being physically present, but taking no real, intellectual or, what is more serious, spiritual part.

Roman Catholics were at last taking seriously the great criticism that we Protestants level at the Catholic liturgy, namely that the sumptuous ceremonial beneath the soaring arches of cathedrals, as well as the Mass itself said on Sundays in a humble village church, are a spectacle, a sort of *tableau vivant* played before a public which, beyond a few automatic gestures, takes no part in it at all. In a popular inquiry conducted in 1946 by the weekly paper *Témoignage chrétien*, one reads the following description of the Mass by a Catholic school-teacher: 'Does the congregation get as much as it should from the Mass? You only have to cast a glance over the vast majority of those present at the celebration to see the true state of affairs. Most are bored and waiting for it to end, watching their neighbours or thinking about their own affairs; some are saying their rosary; a few try to follow in their missals the translations of the prayers which the priest at the altar is reading in Latin. All are there, for what their presence is worth; very few are taking part.'[1]

Against this attendance which is not participation the encyclical *Mediator Dei* protests strongly. Naturally it reaffirms the objective nature of Eucharistic worship, which is concerned with a sacrifice, the sacrifice of the Cross renewed by the priest, who, representing in his person Jesus Christ himself, offers it to God. This sacrifice is valid even when the priest offers it alone, when he says his Mass alone. On this point the encyclical is unequivocal: 'The sacrifice,' it declares, 'is really accomplished . . .; it is in no way necessary that the people should ratify what has been done by the sacred minister.' But when the people are there with the priest they must take part in the Mass. That, says the Pope, 'is their duty and highest privilege'. And he explains that they must take part in the Eucharistic sacrifice 'not passively or negligently or with a distracted mind, but with such active devotion as to be in the closest union with the High Priest . . .' offering 'with him and through him, and with him to surrender themselves'.

Alongside the traditional Roman Catholic affirmations concerning the Mass as a renewal of Christ's sacrifice, and concerning the sacerdotal character of the priest as alone able to offer this sacrifice, one finds in the encyclical *Mediator Dei* certain developments which recall exactly our own Reformed position relative to the Offertory. The people must make the offering with the priest, in union with the priest, but they must also offer themselves. I have referred to the fact that in his first Mass in the vulgar tongue,

[1] *La Maison-Dieu*, No. 11, 1947, III, p. 117.

celebrated in Strasbourg Cathedral in 1523, Theobald Nigri had already gone back to this deep meaning of the Offertory, seeing in it not the offering of the flesh and blood of Christ, but the offering of ourselves, according to the words of St Paul: 'Present your bodies a living sacrifice, holy, acceptable unto God, which is your reasonable service.' In the same perspective the Pope writes: 'The apostle's exhortation requires all Christians, so far as human power allows, to reproduce in themselves the sentiments that Christ had when he was offering himself in sacrifice: sentiments of humility, of adoration. . . . It requires them also to become victims, as it were. . . . It requires us all, in a word, to die mystically with Christ on the Cross, so that we may say with the same apostle: "With Christ I hang upon the Cross." ' Our Reformed liturgies are here in full accord with the pontifical teaching. They all take up, in one form or another, St Paul's words: 'Present your bodies'; they all repeat: 'We offer ourselves unto thee, to be a holy and living sacrifice.'

This communion with Christ in his sacrifice is not, in the encyclical, an idea thrown out in passing; the Pope comes back to it several times, insisting: 'They [the faithful] will consecrate themselves to the glory of God, desiring intensely to make themselves as like as possible to Jesus Christ who suffered so much, and offering themselves as a spiritual victim with and through the High Priest himself.' And elsewhere: 'We thus identify ourselves with Christ as victim for the greater glory of the Eternal Father.' And then there is this formula, taken from St Augustine: 'In the sacrifice she offers, the Church herself is offered.'

The aim of the present liturgical movement, then, is admitted by all—including his Holiness—to be the bringing of the people into more effective participation in the Church's worship, and particularly Eucharistic worship. But by what practical means is this universally desired participation to be achieved?

2. *The position of the priest during the Mass*

It is at this point that we see a prolific outgrowth of experiments of all kinds, essays, innovations, para-liturgies. It was this very exuberance which called forth the encyclical from the Holy See.

Let us take first the question of the position of the priest during the Mass.

It is becoming more and more common for the priest to face the people while he officiates, the better to associate them in the Eucharistic rite. This is the most ancient position—the so-called basilican position. It is the position almost always adopted nowadays when the Mass is celebrated in the open air, for instance in a meeting of Scouts or of the J.O.C. (Jeunesse Ouvrière Catholique, the Catholic workers' youth movement). Some newly-built churches also are designed so that the priest may officiate facing the people. The Liturgical Congress of North America at its last session in London, Ontario, in August, 1956, expressed a desire to see the custom become general: 'That the practice of celebrating the Mass facing the people should be encouraged, as being a practice which has proved to be of great pastoral value in encouraging the participation of the faithful in the Mass.'[1]

From the beginning the Reformation went back to this position of the minister facing the people. It was one of the first innovations in Strasbourg. The priest did not officiate at the altar, which would have obliged him to turn his back on the people. A small table was provided, and the Lord's Supper was celebrated in the midst of the congregation.

The encyclical says nothing about the position of the priest facing the congregation. It is an established fact that it was the original position, and so difficult to condemn. But the Pope attacks exaggerated attachment to ancient rites. 'The liturgy of the early ages,' he says, 'is worthy of veneration; but an ancient custom is not to be considered better . . . just because it has the flavour of antiquity.'

Recalling and explaining this pontifical view, Cardinal Cicognani

---

[1] *La Documentation catholique*, 14th October, 1956, p. 1299. A similar view is taken by some Anglicans. Cf. Basil Minchin, *The Celebration of the Eucharist Facing the People*, The Warden Press, Bristol, 1954.

in his opening speech to the Congress of Assisi declared: 'They would be in error who saw in the various liturgical reforms and restorations . . . a nostalgia for ancient forms, a sort of aesthetically or mystically motivated romanticism, a sentimental attachment to the past; no, certainly not: the chief, and I might say the only reason for these reforms and restorations consists in the burning desire to see the people really living the life of Christ.'[1]

In order to legitimize this relative liberty with regard to the past, the Pope appeals to the great Catholic idea of development, so magnificently stated by Newman, and shows that the transformations of what he calls the human element in the liturgy bear witness to the continuing life of the Church through the centuries, a life which is always germinating afresh. One feels that there is something of a dilemma in all this; the desire at any price to resuscitate the past must be avoided, and so also must the desire to rush too hastily into new paths. The Holy See is seeking a middle way, and cautions against those who hold obstinately to a past that is beyond recall, and at the same time against innovators whose revolutionary haste accords ill with the pace (too slow for their liking) at which the Hierarchy moves.

Although the encyclical does not contain any reference to the basilican position, the Pope's discourse to the members of the international congress at Assisi does allude to it, and appears to approve of the custom, which is becoming more and more widespread. Examining the relationship between the altar and the tabernacle, he recalls the institution of the Holy Office: 'The holy Eucharist must be kept in an irremovable tabernacle placed in the middle of the altar.' To have the tabernacle on the altar might be awkward for celebration facing the people. So the Pope declares: 'The manner in which the tabernacle may be placed on the altar without hindering the celebration facing the people may be solved in various ways, a matter on which the specialists will advise.'[2]

Pius XII seems here to be accepting the basilican position as a matter of course. There seems indeed to have been some evolution

[1] *La Maison-Dieu*, Nos. 47-8, 1956, IV, p. 32.   [2] *Ibid.*, p. 342.

in his thinking since the encyclical *Mediator Dei*, in which the position facing the people is passed over in silence.

3. *The use of the vernacular*

The question of the language of the liturgy is of greater significance. It is on this point that the most spectacular transformation in the Roman Catholic liturgy is taking place.

Active participation by the layman in the Mass requires him to understand what is being done and said. Hence the Masses in dialogue form, with responses in the vulgar tongue, the hymns by the congregation, following with appropriate words the progress of the Mass, and the reading in French of the Epistle and Gospel. I speak mainly of what is being done in my own country.

There are some who would like to go further. The Liturgical Congress of North America passed the following resolution: 'That to increase its pastoral value the Mass of the catechumens should be authorized in the vulgar tongue.'[1] This resolution refers only to the Mass of the Catechumens, the first part of the Mass. There are those who would go further still, and have the entire Mass, including the most sacred prayers of the Canon, said in a language intelligible to all. But on this point the Pope is adamant. While approving the Masses in dialogue form, the responses by the people, and the singing of hymns related to the various parts of the liturgy, he explicitly condemns those who 'in the celebration of the august sacrifice of the Eucharist use the vulgar tongue'.

Nevertheless the question is raised. *Témoignage chrétien*, in a big inquiry answered by two hundred people, from typists, and peasant-girls scarcely able to read, to university graduates, did not hesitate to raise it publicly.[2] Some of the replies received are significant. Take for example this one: 'We smile at the prayer-mills of Asia, but is singing Latin psalms without understanding them much more intelligent?' Or this: 'After all, the words of the

[1] *La Documentation catholique, loc. cit.*
[2] See Martimort, 'Les leçons d'une enquête', in *La Maison-Dieu*, No. 11, 1947, III, pp. 84f.

Mass are not magic incantations.' A teacher in a state school: 'Did Jesus speak to his disciples in a language they could not understand?' One last example, from among many one could quote: 'It is painful to me to see how very far away from us is this God whom we address in Latin.' Is it not significant that it has been possible to write and publish such replies? There is here the beginning of a movement which may in the fairly near future exert pressure on the Hierarchy itself and bring it to depart from the intransigent position which considers Latin as the only language suitable for the celebration of the mysteries.

In any case French is already invading the liturgy. The better to inform myself, I went to see a bishop who was my colleague in the University of Strasbourg, and who honours me with his friendship. He furnished me with a little Ritual authorized by the Sacred Congregation of Rites, in which almost the whole of the liturgy of the Sacraments, prayers, creed and formularies is translated into French; and the preface specifies that the use of these texts in the vulgar tongue is authorized to the extent to which it may seem useful.

Thus, in the service for infant Baptism:

'Que demandez-vous?—La foi.
Que vous procure la foi?—La vie éternelle.'

('What do you seek?—Faith.
What does faith procure for you?—Eternal life.')

The blessing of the salt is to be said in Latin, but its imposition is done in French. The exorcisms are in Latin, as well as the sacramental formula. All the sacramental formulae are in Latin and not translated; but everything else is translated, whatever the Sacrament concerned, except for Ordination, so that the whole ceremony, apart from a few sentences, may be celebrated in French. The same applies to the funeral services.

This seems to me to mark a turning-point in the liturgical life of the Roman Church. 'In many functions,' says the encyclical already referred to, 'the adoption of the vernacular may prove of great benefit to the faithful.' Permission can of course be given only by the Apostolic See. But, as can be seen from the preface of the *Rituale parvum* which I have just mentioned, the concession is made fairly liberally.

There is even a demand for a vernacular version of the Breviary, intended as it is for the priest, who must know Latin. The resolution on this subject passed by the Liturgical Congress of North America is significant: 'That priests in active ministry be authorized to recite the Breviary in their mother-tongue.' The reasons for this request are given:

For the good of the priest. The recitation of the Divine Office in his mother-tongue will contribute greatly to the personal devotion and piety of the priest.

For the priest's preaching. The recitation of the Divine Office in the same language in which he preaches would give the priest a more lively contact with Holy Scripture, the Fathers of the Church, and the writings of the Sovereign Pontiffs, so enriching his preaching.

For the propagation of the faith. The recitation of the Divine Office in the mother-tongue, and the greater familiarity with the Old and New Testaments which would result, would have great pastoral value for the priest in his contacts with those separated from the unity of the Church, particularly in predominantly Protestant countries.[1]

4. *The communion of the laity*

Another sign of the times is the increasingly frequent custom of the laity communicating at the Mass with the priest. The Eucharist, without losing anything of its many-sided significance, is becoming more and more like a meal. 'The bread is eaten,' writes Fr Doncoeur, 'and it is in order to be eaten in a meal that it is given to us in the Eucharist.' With regret he records: 'Modern worship has almost lost sight of the fact that it is a meal at which

[1] *La Documentation catholique*, 14th October, 1956, p. 1301.

one eats.' He comes to the point of protesting against the false mysticism of the 'white Host', against the 'wafers' which to simple eyes are anything but bread. 'If Christ took real bread, what we should call household bread, he had his reasons, and one must believe that he was not much troubled by the scruples which worry us, such as the necessity of chewing it with one's teeth or the danger of dropping crumbs, and so on.' He concludes ironically: 'Doubtless the Host has the virtues of Bristol paper—it will keep for a whole month. Think what slavery it would be if it were necessary to bake it fresh every day. We expect fresh bread for breakfast, but how very unreasonable to expect it for the Communion!'

He protests also against the withholding of the cup from the laity, when for a thousand years Christians used to pass this cup one to another as the apostles themselves did. 'If we prized God's gift so highly that it hurt us to be deprived of it, I cannot believe that the humble tears of the faithful would fail to triumph over such an ill-founded rule.'[1] It is, as I was saying, a sign of the times that it has become possible to say things of this kind. Such pleas have not been heard in the Church since the time of the Reformation. No wonder, then, that the Holy See is putting the brake on hard. The encyclical does declare that it is most desirable that the laity should communicate as well. But it goes on at once to say: 'It is a false doctrine that would lead a priest to refuse to celebrate unless the faithful come to Communion; and it is still worse to ground this view—that the faithful must necessarily communicate together with the priest—on the sophistical contention that the Mass besides being a Sacrifice is also the banquet of a community of brethren; and that the general Communion of the faithful is to be regarded as the culminating point of the whole celebration.'

Nevertheless, in his allocution to the members of the Assisi congress, the Pope appears to be making some concession. Is it

[1] Fr Doncoeur, 'Requêtes fondamentales d'une renaissance liturgique', in *La Maison-Dieu*, No. 25, 1951, I, p. 28.

possible that here too there has been some—perhaps unconscious
—evolution in his thought? He affirms as strongly as ever the
objective character of the sacrifice of the Mass, and refutes the
view, which he describes as erroneous, that the celebration of a
single Mass attended piously by a hundred priests is the equivalent
of a hundred Masses celebrated by a hundred priests. In the light
of the objective character of the Eucharistic sacrifice, one Mass
cannot be equivalent to a hundred Masses, even if these hundred
were each said by a priest on his own, and the single Mass were
attended by an innumerable multitude. It is the more striking to
find that the Sovereign Pontiff, without departing from this
sacramental and dogmatic intransigence, nevertheless refers to the
Eucharist as 'sacrifice and meal'.[1] This is the first time, to my
knowledge, that this double qualification has been given to the
Eucharist in the pontifical annals.

The fact is that the conception of the Eucharist as a feast,
without in any way obscuring the fact that it is a sacrifice, is
gaining ground in the thoughts and habits of Roman Catholics.
One notices it in the increase in communions, whereas the Euchar-
ist-sacrifice is self-sufficient, and does not as such imply the communion of the people. For instance, it has been quite surprising
to see the numbers of Roman Catholics who take part in the Good
Friday Communion which has been established by the new *Ordo*.
This too is a movement full of promise. There has, of course, been
no modification in the traditional doctrine of the Eucharist, but
the conception of a real common meal, so long kept in the background, is beginning to show itself through the dogmatism of
transubstantiation. In the van of this movement are the French
Catholics, who are thus once again showing themselves to be the
enfants terribles of the Church.

5. *The liturgical use of silence*

I come now to another tendency in the present liturgical
movement: the rediscovery of the value of silence.

[1] *La Maison-Dieu*, Nos. 47-8, 1956, IV, p. 332.

In fact all true liturgies include periods of silence. And silence is not an empty space of time: it can be as full as times of speaking and singing. It may be our response to the greatness and majesty of God, an expression of our creatureliness: 'Be silent, O all flesh, before the Lord.' It is associated with the awe we feel when faced with the unfathomable wisdom of God and of his ways. It is, in short, the attitude of contemplation, adoration, and prayer— the prayer which both mounts up towards God, and waits in humility upon him, and which neither seeks nor finds expression in words.

Such a silence is not easily prescribed by rubric; it is the natural growth of habit. Thus, in the Mass, after the *Oremus*, which is all that is left of a prayer now disappeared—for it is not, in fact, followed by a prayer—a period for silent prayer is now often included. The Bishop of Fréjus is seeking to introduce this in his diocese, and the Bishop of Nancy writes: 'Christians who understand the Mass desire a moment of personal prayer, to offer themselves to God.' (Once again this offering, this dedication of ourselves with Christ and in Christ.) 'May they be helped in this,' he adds, 'by the organ, or by silence.'[1]

The organ . . . or silence. If I might make here a plea in respect of the liturgies in my own Church, I would say: silence, and not the organ. Silence to the accompaniment of an organ voluntary is pseudo-silence. One sometimes feels one is in a concert-hall rather than a place of worship. Such improvisations by the organist set us inwardly on edge by their aggressive tonalities or the feeling they give us that he is just practising. Paradoxical though it may be, the organ voluntary must be such that one does not listen to it or hear it; it must be no more than a background of sound, uplifting our prayer without our being aware of it. This is in accord with the view expressed by an eminent Roman Catholic, Henri Ghéon: 'I must make a confession,' he writes; 'the only kind of music I can bear at Mass . . . is a vague organ, banal harmonies and Gregorian chant. They form a sort of bass to my prayers without

---

[1] *La Maison-Dieu*, No. 25, 1951, I, p. 122.

disturbing them. . . . Everything changes at once as soon as there is an *accident*. . . . Without exception everything good or bad that attracts my attention and appeals to my aesthetic sense is an *accident*. Then it requires a superhuman effort to reconcile my pleasure, if the music pleases me (and my displeasure in the opposite case), with my attention to the mystery of the altar.'[1]

This need and desire for silence for individual prayer which is making its appearance in the very heart of the solemnities of the liturgy is a development particularly to be noted.

Of course, the liturgical movement which is taking shape within the Roman Church is not very clearly defined. There are many reforms in the air, so to speak, which have not been translated yet into fact. Some perhaps will be successful; others will be abortive. Its fluidity is one of the characteristics of the liturgical movement at the present time. Everything is in suspense; nothing has taken definite shape. One thing is certain: the growing interest in liturgical matters. There is an increasing realization that the liturgy lies at the heart of the life of the Church, one of its essential tasks. With its rhythm of silences and canticles, of receiving and offering, of aspiration and awe, is it not the lungs with which the Church breathes?

III. OPPOSITION

It can well be imagined that such a movement does not develop without setting up counter-currents. There has been lively opposition. The innovations have come up against a sort of ultra-conservative traditionalism which regards their advocates as dangerous revolutionaries.

The most influential opposition came from Paul Claudel, shortly before his death. In an article in *Figaro littéraire* of 29th January, 1955, he poked fun at what he calls the Mass back to front—the title of his article. The Mass back to front is the Mass

[1] H. Ghéon, *In Search of Mozart*, translated by Alexander Dru, Sheed and Ward, London, 1934, pp. 182-3.

said by the priest facing the people. 'The new liturgy,' he wrote, paradoxically, 'detracts from the dignity and rights of Christian people. It is no longer the people saying the Mass with the priest (who turns towards them from time to time to assure himself of their presence and co-operation) . . . ; all we have is a curious crowd watching the priest at his work. Unbelievers may very well compare him to a juggler performing his act in front of a politely amazed audience.' Naturally Paul Claudel let fly in passing—it would not be Claudel if he did not—a side-kick at Protestantism: 'This deplorable modern custom has completely upset the ancient rite, to the great dismay of faithful Catholics. There is no longer an altar; nothing but a sort of trestle with a cloth on it, which reminds one painfully of the Calvinist bench.' At bottom, what Claudel feared was the suppression, or at the very least the weakening, of the sense of mystery. For him the Eucharist was a mystery which one must not attempt to simplify or explain; he called to witness the iconostasis of Eastern churches, behind which, out of sight of the people altogether, the miracle of transubstantiation takes place.

Claudel's article did not go unanswered. In the *Bulletin de la communauté chrétienne de Saint-Séverin* of 30th January, 1955, it was pointed out to him that the position of the priest facing the people simply marked a return to the original practice of the Church. At the same time the article insisted on the fact that the sacrifice is accomplished only in the sacrament, and that the sacrament of the Eucharist is consummated in a meal. 'The Mass, the sacrifice of Christ, is only realized in the Supper-meal; it is essentially a meal.' There is therefore no question whether the people be in front of the priest or behind him; in this sense there is neither a right-way-round nor a back-to-front Mass. The people are all around: *circumstantes*, as the Canon of the Mass says. 'The people,' the article continues, 'are around the altar as if around a table; they are eating a ritual meal together, and it is this assembly which realizes in its midst, under the species of the bread and wine, the presence of the sacrificed and glorified

Christ.' I have made a point of quoting this article, because it confirms what I was saying about the new concept which is gaining ground in Roman Catholicism: that of the Mass as a communal meal. It is in the congregation of the faithful, in the course of this meal, that the presence of the sacrificed and glorified Christ is manifested. It is a shift of emphasis. The presence of Christ is no longer associated only with the material elements of the sacrament, the transubstantiated bread and wine, and with the sacramental formulae which operate the transubstantiation; it is associated with the ceremony in its entirety, with the meal itself, with the reality of the community and the communion of the faithful.

It is true that in March of this year (1957) Cardinal Feltin, Archbishop of Paris, wrote a letter to the parish priest at Saint-Séverin, asking him to adhere strictly, when celebrating High Mass, to the 'directive' put out by the assembly of cardinals and archbishops of France. The things which he was particularly concerned should be given up were the reading of the Epistle and Gospel in French, the audible recitation of the Prayer of the Canon, and a standing position (as opposed to kneeling) for receiving Communion.

Less precise, but pointing in the same direction, is Fr Roguet's conception. He wishes the Mass to be envisaged as a whole, without the sacramental words being isolated and being made to take all the weight. 'The mystery,' he writes, 'is not to be defined by its limitations, but by its fullness. . . . To penetrate the heart of the mystery of the Mass and to take with us the faithful who are listening to us, we shall not isolate the consecration like some chemical element that we proceed to dissect atomically by means of precise definitions. We shall try to grasp one after the other all the elements with which the liturgy provides us: a most spacious, complete and concrete ceremony, in which are mingled prayers and readings, in which is exercised the priesthood of the whole Church through the assembly and celebration of the community, through its songs and its actions. . . . We read the account of the Last Supper, not in order to isolate from it two sacramental sentences, but in order to discern the whole intention of Christ in the historical and ritual context in which he celebrated that meal.'[1] Though not yet clearly defined, there is here a tendency to diminish the importance of the consecration proper, and to give to the mystery a new dimension, making it coincident, not with a particular moment isolated from its context, but with the rite as a whole. It is only a step further to the conception that the sacramental presence of Christ is linked not to certain formulae but to the Eucharistic synaxis itself. A new road—one which is also, it would seem, the primitive road—is opening out before Roman Catholic piety. If it is followed, transubstantiation—no longer fed by the sap of a living piety—may gradually become a supererogatory dogma. It is true that the Holy See, at any rate up to the present, has set its face against this new doctrine. Pius XII in the discourse with which he closed the Assisi congress insisted, when speaking of concelebration, upon the necessity of the formula of consecration, which remained for him the essential part of the Mass.

At the same time as he protested against the position of the priest facing the people, Claudel inveighed also against the altar transformed into a table or a bench, shorn of all the traditional liturgical ornaments. 'The priest says his Mass in a void. When he invites the people to lift up their hearts and eyes—towards what? There is no longer anything in front of us to serve as a frontispiece to the rising sun.' In *Figaro littéraire* of 5th February a Catholic replied to him: 'If Christ had been born in our time, he would have worn the workman's blue dungarees, and had his last meal on a trestle-table.' He adds: 'The bareness of the modern altar is the bareness of the stable, the bareness of the Cross. . . . Many churches in both town and country would be better off if they made a clean sweep of the elaborate gilded structures around their altars. And when the priest invites the people to lift up their

---

[1] A. M. Roguet, 'Comment annoncer le mystère de la messe', in *La Maison-Dieu*, No. 14, 1948, II, pp. 102-3.

hearts, either their hearts are no more lifted up than are their bodies, comfortably installed in their pews, or else they are lifted in gladness high above the gilt—higher even than the Cross—to God, to whom the sacrifice is offered.'

There remains the question of the mystery. Paul Claudel wanted worship to be a mystery. He rejected everything that smacked of explanation or translation into a modern idiom. The incomprehensible is part of the mystery. Other voices join with his: 'The invasion of the rational into worship is a symptom of decadence of faith, and may well become one of its causes. . . . It is in the nature of liturgical language to be mysterious. . . . Ours is a religion of mysteries.'[1]

To which it is easy to reply—and the reply was made—that Latin is not a mysterious language to those who understand it, and that its use leaves a whole host of people, apart from a few initiates, in ignorance, thus turning Christianity into an esoteric religion. And in any case, the mystery does not reside in the formulae of the liturgy, which have nothing magic about them, but in the facts of the religion themselves, in God's unimaginable gift to us of his Son Jesus Christ, and in Christ's gift of himself made in the Eucharist. 'Our Christianity,' wrote one priest cogently enough, 'contains enough mysteries already, without our adding arbitrarily to them.'[2]

A schoolteacher declared: 'I am struck by the interest taken by my non-Christian colleagues in Protestant funerals. How they listen as the pastor speaks of the eternal verities! . . . Whereas they have nothing but scorn for liturgical gestures which remind one of magical rites, and for prayers said in a language they do not understand.'[3]

Clearly Paul Claudel's view is far from being general. His article, which made something of a stir, aroused deeply-felt reactions. One suspects that the dyke he was trying to set up

[1] 'La leçon d'une enquête', in *La Maison-Dieu*, No. 11, 1947, III, pp. 88-9.
[2] *Ibid.*, p. 96.   *Ibid.*, p. 115.

against the current is already submerged, if not actually swept away.

IV. THE NEW ORDER OF HOLY WEEK

I come now to the new *Ordo* of Holy Week.[1] We shall have occasion to note in it the appearance of trends of a somewhat different kind, which lie behind the decisions of the Hierarchy.

Firstly, there is the desire to follow the events of Holy Week more closely in the ceremonies which commemorate them. From this point of view it is a restoration of the ancient forms of the Passiontide liturgy. St Augustine records that in his day the principal mysteries of our redemption were celebrated 'on the same days of the week, and at the same hours, when these most holy mysteries had taken place'.[2] But towards the close of the Middle Ages these ceremonies, which took place in the afternoon or at night, were brought forward to the early morning. As long as Maundy Thursday and Good Friday were holidays people still came to the services; but when they became ordinary working-days attendance at the services was greatly reduced.

The new Order is concerned with:

1. *The times of the services in Holy Week.* On Palm Sunday the solemn blessing of the palms and the procession are to take place at the accustomed hour in the morning. The Maundy Thursday Mass, called *In Coena Domini,* is to be celebrated in the evening and not in the afternoon, since it was in the evening that the Lord's Supper was instituted. On Good Friday the commemoration of the Saviour's death is celebrated at about three o'clock, or at any rate not after six o'clock, since it was at the ninth hour (three in the afternoon) that Christ gave up the Ghost. The Paschal vigil is also to be celebrated in the evening, so that the solemn Mass of the Vigil will begin at about midnight between Holy Saturday and

---

[1] English version: *Holy Week Book in Latin and English, according to the Ordo Hebdomadae Sanctae Instauratus,* C. Goodliffe Neale, Birmingham, 1956.

[2] *Epistles,* LV, 14.

Easter Day. One sees in all these arrangements an evident desire to follow more closely when commemorating them the actual course of the historical events of the Passion.

2. *The Palm Sunday Procession.* The new *Ordo* seeks to restore the triumphal and popular character which this ceremony once had. Red, the colour of triumph, is the prescribed liturgical colour. The procession must not be reduced to a mere token, but should be made if possible from a second church or a chapel to the principal church, through the streets of the town. At the very least it must go all round the church. The aim of this rubric is to restore to the procession a character of authenticity which it had lost. On the other hand, the rite of the blessing of the palms is reduced to the simplest possible form. What matters is not this secondary rite, however popular devotion may cherish it, but the procession acclaiming Christ the King, like the multitudes on the road from the Mount of Olives. It is thus the purpose of the *Ordo* to go back to the essentials of the liturgy, at the expense of some of the parasitic excrescences and additions so dear to the popular mind. As in the old *Ordo* the Mass of the Passion follows the procession. To say it the priest changes his vestments; the liturgical colour is violet.

3. *The Mass called 'In Coena Domini'.* The old *Ordo* said simply: *Si erit habendus sermo.* The new *Ordo* reads: *Valde convenit . . .* 'It is most appropriate that a homily should be preached on the great mysteries which are commemorated in this Mass.' Here we have the reintroduction of the sermon into the liturgy of the Mass, not as an obligation, but as most appropriate. 'On this account,' notes a Roman Catholic theologian, 'the new Holy Thursday rubric takes on a particular importance.'[1] The possibility of celebrating the rite of the washing of feet is similarly provided for.

4. *Good Friday.* Whereas formerly the laity did not communicate on the Friday in Holy Week, now they are invited to do so in the course of the solemn liturgical action in the afternoon. In this the *Ordo* rejoins the practice of certain Protestant Churches

[1] *La Maison-Dieu*, No. 45, 1956, I, p. 27.

(the Lutherans in particular) for which Good Friday is the greatest Communion day of the year. This office is not a Mass, and those who communicate partake of the Hosts consecrated the previous day.

5. *The Vigil of Easter.* It is the Mass of this Vigil which constitutes the true Mass of the Easter *triduum*, since on Good Friday and Holy Saturday there is no proper Mass. This Easter watch becomes the climax of all the Holy Week commemorations. It is now that there takes place the blessing of the Paschal candle, which represents the Saviour himself, the light of the world. There takes place also the blessing of the baptismal water, in memory of the Baptism of the catechumens which was celebrated in the ancient Church during the night preceding Easter morning.

This, in broad outline, is the new Order of Holy Week. It is marked by a very clear tendency to have the various rites of the week coincide with the actual course of the historical events of the Passion, and also to prune the liturgy in order to bring out what is essential. The Easter Vigil, in particular, is a happy innovation. It is to be hoped that the Mass of the Paschal Vigil will be celebrated with as much zeal, thanksgiving, and joy as the Christmas Midnight Mass, and Easter Day as gladly as Christmas Day.

V. EVENING MASS AND NEW RULES FOR FASTING

The new ordering of Holy Week has reinstated the Communion of the laity. The same aim was pursued by the Holy See in the Apostolic Constitution *Christus Dominus*, of 6th January, 1953. Under certain conditions it authorized the practice of evening Mass, permitting for the purpose some relaxation in the rules for fasting, so that Communion may be given at these evening celebrations, thus achieving full participation by the laity in the Eucharistic mystery. It is therefore possible from now on to communicate at evening Mass. An abstinence from liquids of one hour's duration is sufficient (this does not apply to water, which is still permitted, nor to alcoholic beverages, which are still forbidden); from solid food, an abstinence of three hours will suffice.

This decision is motivated by considerations of two kinds. Firstly, spiritual considerations: the growing appetite of the laity for the Eucharist, to which the Constitution gives new opportunities for satisfaction, while at the same time setting out to encourage it. Secondly, social considerations: conditions of work have undergone considerable modification in modern times. The time for recreation and leisure is usually the late afternoon and evening, whereas the morning in most homes is a rush to be in time to start the day's work. On the other hand, it is difficult on a Sunday, after the hard work of the week, to keep up the fast until midday, in order to be able to communicate at the High Mass. This threatened to weaken, if not to destroy, all Eucharistic life in those who had not the courage—or perhaps the health—to fast for the required time. It is now therefore possible for the laity to communicate at an evening Mass, three hours only after a meal or one hour after drinking a substantial liquid. (A substance is defined as liquid when it flows, and the spoon will not stand upright by itself in it.) 'There were some souls,' declared Mgr Garrone at the Assisi congress, 'who perhaps without knowing it were hungry for the Eucharist, and who realized the fact on the day when the Sovereign Pontiff showed them the Bread within their reach, in the framework of their life as it is organized (or disorganized) in the conditions of today. He has prepared a table before us, we may say, in the midst of a seemingly "enemy" world (Ps. 23).'[1]

Though the Apostolic Constitution relaxes the rules for fasting, it does not abolish it. Fasting is not made necessary because of the respect due to the Body of the Lord, which must not be mixed with other foods. Nor is it the result of any necessity of imposing bodily penance upon oneself in order to receive it worthily. The reason for the guard which for centuries the Church has mounted

---

[1] G. Garrone, 'Portée pastorale de la Constitution *Christus Dominus*', in *La Maison-Dieu*, Nos. 47-8, 1956, IV, p. 216.

about the Eucharistic meal, is—according to Mgr Garrone—to defend it from being confused with an ordinary meal. According to another liturgist the reason is quite the contrary—to make the Communion like a true meal. 'The Eucharist,' he writes, 'is, and must remain, a meal. Meals are normally eaten fasting, that is to say after the preceding meal has been digested.'[1]

Whatever the motives of the Roman Church for maintaining the discipline of the Eucharistic fast, it is now very much eased. The result has been immediate. In France as in England, according to the information collected by Mgr Garrone, the celebration of an evening Mass on holidays of obligation is now a general practice, and attendance at this Mass is four or five times greater than that at the morning Mass when it was the only one celebrated. We may suppose that the number of communicants has increased in proportion. In many parishes, moreover, there is an evening Mass not only on holidays of obligation but also on Sundays, and on the first Friday in the month. There one may see mothers who in the morning are kept at home looking after their children, office-workers and tradespeople who are not at liberty in the morning, and old people who have long been of necessity deprived of the Sunday service, happy to be able to attend it in the evening. Mgr Garrone affirms that these are but the first signs of a profound change which has not yet by any means revealed all that it portends.[2]

VI. THE WORD OF GOD AND TRADITION

This review of the present trends of the liturgical movement in Roman Catholicism would be incomplete without a mention of

[1] H. R. Philippeau, 'Nouvelle discipline du jeûne eucharistique', in *La Maison-Dieu*, No. 13, 1948, I, p. 85.

[2] *Op. cit.*, p. 220. *Translator's note:* By a *motu proprio* entitled *Sacram Communionem*, dated 19th March, 1957, the Pope authorizes bishops to permit the celebration of Mass after midday on any day. In addition, the modified rules for fasting (three hours' abstinence from solid food, and one hour from liquids) are extended to all Masses, whenever celebrated. These new rulings came into force on 25th March, 1957.

the Biblical revival, and in consequence the increased attention paid to preaching. The evidence of this revival is considerable. I have had occasion to make several quotations from the Congress of Assisi, which was held from the 18th to the 22nd September, 1956, and whose official proceedings were published in *La Maison-Dieu*. There were no discussions, properly so-called, nor were any decisions taken, because of the hierarchical character of the congress. The aim was simply to draw the conclusions following from the liturgical measures of Pius XII, and in particular the encyclical *Mediator Dei*. Fr Roguet addressed the congress on the liturgical revival and the revival in preaching,[1] while the Rev. Fr Béa spoke of the pastoral value of the Word of God in the liturgy.[2] It is striking to hear Catholic theologians speaking today of the Word of God in terms that might be used by the sons of the Reformation, giving back its sovereign importance to the Bible. 'The holy books,' Fr Béa asserted, 'are the Word of God. . . . In them it is not man that speaks—it is the Holy Spirit.' He concluded, in a reference to the encyclical of Pius XII, *Divino afflatu Spiritu*, that 'every move to make the Scriptures better known, read, studied and used, deserves our best praise, our full approval, and sincere encouragement'.[3]

Much more, the Word of God is put on a level with the Eucharist itself. The spiritual bread of the holy Word is considered as necessary to the life of the soul as is the bread of the Eucharist. One even hears of 'the mystical union between the Word of God and the Bread of Life'; the priest is frequently defined as *Minister Verbi* as well as *Minister Sacramenti*. With the *Imitation of Christ*, Fr Béa sees two tables set up in the Church. One is the table of the altar, on which is placed the consecrated bread, the precious Body of Christ; the other is the table on which lies the holy book of God's Word. Today, he declares, the Sovereign Pontiff 'is concerned to lead the faithful laity also to the second table which the Lord has prepared for them'.[4]

---

[1] *La Maison-Dieu*, Nos. 47-8, 1956, IV, p. 149.
[2] *Ibid.*, p. 127.   [3] *Ibid.*, p. 139.   [4] *Ibid.*, pp. 147-8.

Word and Sacrament—the very message of the Reformation! After having for long subordinated the Sacrament to the Word, the Reformed Churches are rediscovering the true value of the Sacrament. The Roman Catholic Church, after having for long subordinated the Word to the Sacrament, is rediscovering in its turn the true value of the Word.

It is significant that Catholic theologians are attempting, in the wake of the theologians of the Reformed Church, to study more deeply the importance of the ministry of the Word. To the following propositions, for instance, culled from an article in *La Maison-Dieu*, I could make no objection: they might easily come from Protestant writings:

1. God's Word is not only a word about God, but the Word which comes from God, a Word which is God himself inasmuch as in it he expresses himself to his creatures.

2. God's Word cannot be mere verbiage, capricious or lacking in effect. It cannot do other than make real the presence, power, and gift of God.

3. God's Word is concerned less with what God is in himself than with what it is his will to be for his creatures, less with his nature than with his purpose and his acts. It is concerned as much with men as with God—neither God independently of man, nor man independently of God.

4. To the ever-present, eternal aspect of the divine action of the Word, corresponds its historical aspect. The Word of God has been seen and heard; it has lived in human history. It became a fact, an event.

5. Concretely, the Word of God is the whole Christ: his Person and teaching, his work, his death and his Resurrection, for in the whole historical fact of Jesus Christ God has spoken in fullness.

6. God's Word continues to speak to men in Jesus Christ, who is the expression of God's eternal loving-kindness. The mission of the historical Church is to bear witness to Jesus Christ, to turn the eyes of the generations of men towards him, in order to

individualize and make real in time the message of God to men.[1]

In the same issue of *La Maison-Dieu* Fr Bouyer, also speaking of God's Word, declares: 'It must take hold of him [the priest] in the same form as it appears and ever remains in the Bible: as a dialogue in which God in person speaks personally to every man; as an act in which his personal Word itself seizes in its own unique way upon everything that can come into men's minds, in order finally, as it becomes incarnate, to take possession of their lives, the whole of their beings, body and soul.'[2] Like Fr Béa, he goes so far as to affirm that the bread of the Word of God is as necessary as the bread of the Eucharist—further, that the Eucharistic bread would be of no avail if it were not accompanied by the bread of God's Word: 'The very flesh of Christ would be of no use to us if the man of God, the man of Christ, did not first distribute to us on his behalf the words which are spirit and life, so that faith opening our hearts, the Spirit of Christ which enters them with the flesh of Christ may give them life.'[3] It is possible to see in such affirmations a sort of echo of the teaching of the Reformers, who said that the preaching of the Word must accompany the administration of the Sacraments.

Such is the present state—in a few outstanding personalities, it is true, rather than in the general body of church members— of the Biblical revival in the Roman Catholic Church. God's Word is clothed once more in its value and authority. Not only are the Scriptures themselves being disseminated in excellent editions which even our own pastors do not hesitate to use—I am thinking in particular of the Jerusalem Bible, or that of Maredsous—but they are being studied, explored, and loved. Who, if he did not know, would hesitate to take these words, from the pen of Fr Bouyer, to be an exhortation to his students by one of our own Protestant professors of theology: 'Let us make God's Word the

[1] A. Liégé, 'Contenu et pédagogie de la prédication chrétienne', in *La Maison-Dieu*, No. 39, 1954, II, pp. 24ff.

[2] L. Bouyer, 'Conditions d'une prédication pastorale', in *La Maison-Dieu*, No. 39, 1954, IV, p. 52.

[3] *Ibid.*, p. 55.

whole of our inner life, in order to make it the whole of our ministry'?[1]

But, it may be asked, what is happening to tradition in all this? This is indeed the chief complaint made by Protestants against Catholicism, that 'you speak respectfully of the Word of God; you give it an important place—but you are not men of God's Word only. Alongside the Bible you bring in tradition, and so devalue the Word of God instead of honouring it.'

It is true that Catholics continue to speak of tradition. The Pope, in his discourse to the Congress of Assisi, reminded his hearers that the *depositum fidei*, Christian truth, was contained in Scripture and in tradition.[2] Fr Bouyer, too, speaks of tradition in the article quoted: 'The Bible, if it is not to be at the mercy of our caprice, as a dead letter, must never be divorced from the tradition in which its contents remain alive.'[3] But what is meant by tradition?

If tradition constitutes alongside the Bible an independent source of knowledge; if the Bible needs to be supplemented by tradition; then tradition becomes a datum different from that of the Bible, and may enter into competition with it. It is in virtue of this so-called complementary knowledge that there have developed within the Roman Church such things as Mariolatry, the cult of the saints, and the doctrine of Purgatory. It would appear that it is in this sense that Pius XII speaks of it when he sees in Scripture and in tradition the deposit of faith. In saying this he is the faithful guardian of what one might call historical Catholicism. Possibly he considered such a call to order necessary, in face of what he felt were the too one-sided assertions of Frs Béa and Roguet, who in their addresses at Assisi breathed not a single word about tradition. This confirms what I was saying about the fluidity of the movements which are now manifesting themselves within Roman Catholicism. There is a certain tension between the

[1] L. Bouyer, 'Conditions d'une prédication pastorale', in *La Maison-Dieu*, No. 39, 1954, IV, p. 58.
[2] *La Maison-Dieu*, Nos. 47-8, 1956, IV, p. 331.
[3] L. Bouyer, *op. cit.*, p. 52.

conservative tendencies of Roman circles, and the dynamism—in some respects reformative—of certain theologians who are for the most part French. Will they eventually influence the Curia? Or will the latter impose silence upon them? Not by any means all the stakes have yet been laid; and that is what makes the history of our time in these matters so vitally interesting.

It is worth noting that, at least in his article, Fr Bouyer's understanding of tradition is not the same as that reaffirmed by the Pope. For Fr Bouyer tradition is not a source of knowledge alongside the Bible: it is the living environment thanks to which the Bible is not a dead letter, but retains its warmth and its power to shine out. Tradition here does not supplement the Bible, but interprets it at each moment of history; it is as it were the atmosphere through which God's Word comes to us: it is, in Fr Bouyer's own words, 'the treasure of living interpretation in which the mystery which is at the heart of the Divine Word blossoms and becomes explicit, at the same time being continually renewed and made real.' In fact Fr Bouyer is thinking particularly here of the liturgy as being the tradition through which God's Word comes to us. But one may take his words in a wider sense as referring to the living tradition which is the very life of the Church.

Are we Protestants so far from this conception? Is there not, in our case also, a tradition at work—the tradition which is the Church, bearing us along and living in us, perhaps without our knowing it? Of course we react against calling it tradition, but is it not in the light of our own tradition that we read and interpret the Bible? As they reach us through our Reformed atmosphere, are not the rays of the Gospel light refracted in a way that is peculiar to us? The objectivity of the divine revelation in Jesus Christ is in a sense absolute, but our apprehension of it—Reformed, Lutheran, Anglican, Roman Catholic, Orthodox—is always in a sense relative because of our individual traditions. This is inevitable, given our human, social, historical and denominational limitations. It is actually a powerful force towards unity—not the impoverished unity of the least common denominator, but an ecumenical enrichment of us all, as we learn to see what traditions different from our own have seen in the Bible or heard of the Divine Word, the complementary rays of light which they have seen but to which we have remained blind. Thus I am persuaded that Catholics will find in the Bible new aspects of the truth, which we, because of our particular traditions, have not discovered there. They cannot read the Bible in the climate of the Reformation any more than we can read it in the climate of Catholicism, even though it is the same Bible for all. We have need of each other, just as our personal beliefs have need of the synthesis which our own Church makes of them in its creeds, so that we may come together into the light of the truth.

I stress the subject of tradition, because in our opposition to Catholicism we have neglected and underestimated its importance. The Bible is sufficient, we said. But what we did not see was that the Bible was what it was for us only because it was brought to us by a living tradition, that it was the Word of God for us only when set in the great current of spiritual life which proceeds from Christ, and that without that life, outside that life, it would be dead.

Let us imagine that the books of the New Testament had not gone beyond the circle of those to whom they were immediately addressed; that Theophilus had kept to himself the communications of his friend Luke; that Paul's letters had lain untouched in the archives of local churches; that the Judaizers had paralysed his efforts and ruined his work; that the Gospels had been written and then lost, and that Christianity had been finally blotted out in the year 70. There had never been a Christian Church.

And then, twenty centuries later, by a lucky stroke of his pick in the ruins of some city in Asia Minor, an archaeologist has brought to light Paul's Epistles, the Fourth Gospel and the Synoptic Gospels. Do you imagine that on the strength of these old parchments men would at once create churches in Christ's name, that cathedrals would be built, and that the great current of Christian life would begin to flow through the world of men's souls? That would be to attribute to the book a virtue which it alone could not possibly have; it is only amid life that it lives, and if today it is still capable of promoting life, that is because it is perpetually enlivened by contact with the spiritual life of the Christian community.

This *reductio ad absurdum* suffices to show how inescapable tradition is. On this point we are not so far as we appear to be —or as we should like to think we are—from some Catholic theologians. I do not say from official Roman Catholicism, in which another view prevails, one that is to say the least debatable. If the views of these theologians finally prevail, a great step forward will have been made towards ecumenism. The conception of tradition approved by the Council of Trent might then be weakened, like a branch that withers and dies, and the Roman Catholic Church might, instead of a tradition which sets itself up alongside the Gospel as its rival, and even sometimes opposing it, accept a tradition which is not an additional source of knowledge outside the Bible, but which is as it were the great river of Christian life bringing to men's minds—with a slightly differing coloration in each of our confessions—the true revelation of God, the living Word of the living God.

The Biblical revival cannot fail to influence Roman Catholic preaching. If the priest is minister of the Word as well as of the Sacrament, he must proclaim God's Word; hence his role as a preacher. The following propositions bring out clearly the indissoluble link, recognized by certain Roman Catholic theologians, between preaching and the Word of God.

1. All Christian preaching must be done in full consciousness of its complete and fundamental dependence on the Apostolic preaching which is God's Word, and which is the basis of all its authority.

2. The ministry of the word must be subservient entirely and exclusively to the Word of God.

3. The exclusive content of the ministry of the word will be the Word of God.

4. The divine Word fixed by Scripture must not remain a

dead letter. The only way of avoiding this is for a man, one who is involved in all the cares and preoccupations of other men, but one who is at the same time a man of God, to be himself continually remaking the connection between the reality of their daily lives and the eternal reality which is the life of the divine Word.

5. The preacher is first and foremost the messenger of God's Word.

6. The content of true Christian preaching is what God wills to put in the mouth of those whom he makes his witnesses and his prophets among men.[1]

Fr Bouyer sees the preacher as a herald, proclaiming to the people a decree by their king, duly authenticated by the seal of his authority. Echoing the words of the New Testament, he asserts that the ministry of the word is the proclamation of the Kingdom or Reign of God. No Evangelical theologian could object to his definition of what a sermon should be: 'It is not for us to make known our own ideas, nor even some abstract doctrine: we have news to tell, the greatest news, the *good* news.'[2]

In the Roman Church it seems that the ministry of the word has long been neglected, relegated to a secondary role, almost crowded out by the attention paid to the celebration of the mysteries. There was only 'the poorest of sermonettes . . .' which was only 'transfigured by the saving radiance of the Eucharistic miracle', as Karl Barth says.[3] It seems that today Roman Catholic thought—I do not dare to say Roman Catholic practice—is giving back to the sermon the importance it once had, and that this is in fact one of the results of the liturgical movement. The liturgical movement has aroused the interest and the curiosity of the laity concerning the holy mysteries, and created an eager demand for instruction and preaching about them. Some have gone so far as to assert that the ministry of the word is a necessary adjunct to the

---

[1] *La Maison-Dieu*, No. 16, 1948, IV, pp. 36, 46; No. 39, 1954, III, p. 23.

[2] *La Maison-Dieu*, No. 16, 1948, IV, p. 20.

[3] K. Barth, *The Word of God and the Word of Man*, translated by Douglas Horton, Hodder and Stoughton, London, 1928, p. 113.

celebration of the Sacraments, which without it remain opaque and impenetrable, and which need to be 'illuminated'. 'However clear, however free of superfluous matter the rites may be,' said Fr Roguet at the Assisi congress, 'they are still *mysteries* into which we can penetrate only by faith. And faith needs to be illuminated and formed by the word.'[1]

On the other hand it is not forgotten that the Word was made flesh, and consequently that the ministry of the word must be centred on Christ: the whole Word of God is Jesus Christ. We might say that what is taking place is a 'refocussing' of the ministry of the word, so as to remove all the many inessentials that were blurring and obstructing the clear view of its one proper subject, the Person of Christ. 'The basis of our preaching,' said Fr Sertillanges, 'is the eternal Gospel, the good news which the world has received, but has never heard in its fullness, and which it has forgotten. It falls to Christ's heralds to proclaim it aloud to this disjointed, topsy-turvy and spiritually disordered age, over which hangs the threat of fearful destruction.'[2]

It cannot be denied that from the ecumenical point of view this conception of the ministry of the word among certain Roman Catholic writers represents a big step forward. It means that preaching is now viewed from the same angle and in the same light as we Protestants view it. Some go so far as to appeal to the doctrine of the Holy Spirit in order to express the mystery of the ministry of the word. The Word of God becomes real and living for us only if God himself speaks to us. 'If God did not speak to us,' writes Fr Bouyer, 'the things of which his Word speaks to us would lose all meaning. As soon as he speaks to us and by virtue of his speaking to us, what he says to us becomes, for us also, a truth that we can grasp: we are in communication, in communion with the Father through the Son.'[3]

---

[1] *La Maison-Dieu*, Nos. 47-8, 1956, IV, p. 152.

[2] 'L'Esprit de la prédication apostolique', in *La Maison-Dieu*, No. 16, 1948, IV, p. 10.

[3] 'Prédication et mystère', in *La Maison-Dieu*, No. 16, 1948, IV, p. 22.

It is of course within the Church that the Holy Spirit is at work, and that God speaks. Here, as always, the Catholic avoids anything that smacks of individual inspiration. God, when he speaks, always addresses himself only to the Church. The Church alone can pass on God's Word, because she alone can hear it. This is the basis of what has been called the hierarchical character of the ministry of the word, which can be practised only by a mind 'in tune (like the lyre-string, as Ignatius put it) with the bishop'.[1] Again it is defined by Fr Daniélou: 'Transmission through the Church of the Word of God.'[2] The believer will receive God's Word, which is to feed his inner life, from the mouth of the Church. Thus the ministry of the word has no meaning except through the Church and in the Church. Only there is it capable of making its full revelation. Properly speaking, the Word of God is only ever spoken in this world by the Church to the Church. Although the new conception of the role of the ministry of the word is restricted and limited in this way, such limitations should not blind us to the value and the profound significance of the new conception itself.

Has the ministry of the word then in fact been reinstated in the Roman Church, and is it now being practised in conformity with the theories enunciated above? It is difficult to judge. The truth probably is that this theoretical restoration of the ministry of the word contains more of promise for the future than of reform already achieved. I am led to this conclusion by the criticisms now being made on all sides, of the present state of preaching, and the very lively sense of the need for reform felt by the keenest minds of our time. *La Maison-Dieu* records that 'people everywhere are beginning to be anxious about the lack of interest on the part of Christian folk in the preaching of the Word of God as practised in the majority of our pulpits.'[3] The *Nouvelle Revue*

[1] M. Piccari, 'Le caractère hiérarchique de la prédication', *ibid*., p. 68.
[2] Quoted by Jean-Marie Hum, 'Le prêtre, ministre de la parole', in *La Maison-Dieu*, No. 39, 1954, III, p. 131.
[3] 'La crise de la prédication', in *La Maison-Dieu*, No. 13, 1948, I, p. 104.

théologique devoted its June, 1947, issue to 'Preaching and Preachers'. In its leading article, on 'The Sermon from the Hearer's Point of View', the anonymous author points out that the congregation wants to understand the sermons it hears. He quotes this reply given by a peasant to St Francis de Sales, who, after a very learned sermon, had asked him if he had understood it: 'Oh, sir! I was delighted not to understand a word of it. It made me so deeply aware of the mysteries of our holy religion!' No one today would be so easily satisfied not to understand. It is true that the general run of churches, and especially Gothic ones, were not built with the preaching of sermons in mind, so that frequently the preacher's voice scarcely reaches the men-folk massed around the holy-water stoup at the back of the church, so that they are encouraged to slip out into the churchyard for a quiet smoke with the choir-men.

There are other less material obstacles. Sometimes ministers take advantage of the fact that they cannot be answered back, and are severer than they ought to be, or else let themselves go with a gusto that is quite out of place. The author of the article I mentioned goes on to denounce the unreality of many sermons, their intellectual pretentiousness, their excessive use of quotations from the early Fathers, and so on. 'Who are these Fathers of the Church,' he asked one day, 'with whom our parish priest seems to be in such close relations?' The replies were disarming. Some thought they were the clergy of neighbouring parishes; others inclined to the opinion that they were (*sic!*) the dead in the graveyard. One, however, who had been educated in a Catholic college, asserted that the Fathers of the Church were the churchwardens; and, lastly, there was one—very sure of himself—who said that they were the Redemptorists, a party of these good fathers having recently preached a mission in the parish![1]

The charge of unreality is also made against Roman Catholic preaching by Fr Congar: it is not 'a living answer to the questions

---

[1] 'La crise de la prédication', in *La Maison-Dieu*, No. 13, 1948, I, p. 107.

and needs of men', it does not make people 'think about what matters', it is not adapted to 'the real needs of real men'.[1] Fr Bouyer compares priests unfavourably with Protestant pastors in that it is only exceptionally that they go into their pulpits after a preparation worthy of the name, since they do not feel the sermon to be important. If, however, they do take their preaching seriously, they are then prevented from proclaiming God's Word because they still have the ingenuous idea that they must at all costs at that point deliver themselves of a host of other matters.[2]

In his book *L'offensive des sectes*, Fr Chéry quotes a number of opinions put forward by lay-people concerning Catholic sermons: 'Botched, ill-prepared sermons, an out-of-date style, clichés, outworn illustrations. . . . I am ready to receive the seed, not the wind. . . . Nobody listens to sermons. People are tired of being given moral uplift instead of instruction regarding dogma and its applications. It is a pity there is so little reference to the Bible and above all to the New Testament, and that not enough is said about Christ and the great mysteries. We are exasperated by the excessive intrusion of money-matters and such like things.'[3] He diagnoses the attraction of the non-Catholic sects as being largely in their clear and direct preaching, within the understanding of all, with abundant quotations from the Bible, and he makes a strong plea for the reform of preaching in the Roman Church. It must be a *kerygma*, the proclamation in the King's name of the message of salvation. He concludes: 'The ministry of the word is not out of date. What is out of date is the religious orator, the "purveyor of vague things" (Aldous Huxley). The man who has something great and true to say to his fellows will never be out of date.'[4]

[1] 'Pour une liturgie et un prédication réelles', in *La Maison-Dieu*, No. 16, 1948, IV, pp. 84, 86.

[2] 'Conditions d'une prédication pastorale', in *La Maison-Dieu*, No. 39, 1954, III, pp. 43-4.

[3] H. C. Chéry, *L'offensive des sectes*, Editions du Cerf, Paris, 1954, p. 456.

[4] *Ibid.*, p. 464.

The ministry of the word, like the liturgy in the vulgar tongue, has, however, its determined opponents, for whom the mystery is enough; not the mystery of the Word, but that of the Sacraments. The ministry of the word seems to them to be no more than useless verbiage, adding nothing to the Eucharist and even obscuring its essential meaning. Such, for example, is Mauriac, whose mind is nevertheless very open on other points, though closed on the question of sermons. 'A good priest,' he writes, 'has nothing to say to me. I watch him, and that is enough for me. The liturgy is enough for me as well: it is a silent sermon. The religious order that speaks best about God is that of the Benedictines, because they never go into a pulpit. . . . How sorry I am for the Protestants, whose worship is nothing but words! The holy liturgy is the only sermon that touches and persuades me. There is not a single preacher with whom I do not find myself in disagreement by the time he has uttered three sentences.'[1]

Such voices are on the whole isolated; they betray an automatic anti-Protestant reaction, which is very strong in certain quarters, just as automatic anti-Catholicism is in others. They must nevertheless be listened to, to remind us again that the day is far from being won. As in the modernist crisis, it only needs the pontifical pilot to put the tiller of St Peter's ship hard over for everything to be stiffened and stopped. There may be in the Roman Catholic Church signs of a thaw, and a certain fluidity, but everything could be frozen up again the moment it appeared dangerous to the Holy See.

For the moment the movement towards the restoration of the ministry of the word is gaining strength. Cardinal de Salièges, who died recently, devoted one of his last pastoral instructions, in September, 1956, to the duty of preaching. He said: 'The priest who throws himself with ardour into his work, and yet does not find time to preach, is guilty of a grave dereliction of duty. Christ did not say to his disciples: Put on shows, organize outings. He did not even say: Found orphanages and hospitals. He said:

[1] *La Table ronde*, No. 12, December, 1948, p. 1996.

Preach! The apostles understood him well. They left the admin-istration of charity to the deacons, and devoted themselves to the ministry of the Word.' He stresses the duty of priests to make every effort to prepare themselves to speak in public. He wishes them to learn to read properly, to articulate and make themselves heard clearly at a distance.

There can be no doubt that sermons heard on the wireless have led people increasingly to demand a more direct and sub-stantial ministry of the word. Protestant preaching in particular has had no small effect in this respect. I have been told of a certain village priest who, before Mass, collects a few of his parishioners around his wireless set to listen to the Protestant service. The evangelical sermon, clear, direct, inspired throughout by the Bible, has not been without effect on the desire for a revival of the ministry of the word felt by so many Roman Catholics today.

It was to meet this desire that Fr Béa at the Congress of Assisi expressed a wish to see increased the number of 'preaching pericopes', at present too restricted, either by the introduction of a triennial or quadrennial cycle, or by some other device suited to the special needs and circumstances of our times.[1]

The North American Liturgical Congress expressed at about the same time a similar desire: 'That there should be for use at Mass a cycle of readings spread over three or four years, which would give the people an opportunity of getting to know better both the Old and the New Testaments.'[2]

Nevertheless—and this is recognized by those priests whose understanding of spiritual matters is deepest—a ministry of the word that was truly a ministry of the Word of God, could not result from some superficial effort. The preacher himself must be nurtured in God's Word, so that it has become 'as it were, flesh of his flesh, spirit of his spirit, exactly as the Eucharistic bread must become flesh of his flesh and spirit of his spirit'.[3] For God's

---

[1] *La Maison-Dieu*, Nos. 47-8, 1956, IV, p. 142.

[2] *La Documentation catholique*, 14th December, 1956, p. 1300.

[3] A. Béa, in *La Maison-Dieu*, Nos. 47-8, p. 144.

Word may be darkened and lose its power as it passes through a dull mind, just as it can be enlivened as it passes through a lively mind. This was admirably expressed by that modern prophet, Charles Péguy:

'Jesus has not given us dead words,
  For us to shut them up in little boxes (or in big ones),
  Or to preserve them in rancid oil,
  Like Egyptian mummies.
Jesus Christ, my child, has not given us words
To be kept in tins,
But he has given us living words,
To be fed. . . .
So we must feed them; we are to feed in our hearts
With our own flesh and blood,
Those eternal Words, uttered in the flesh. . . .
It is to us, weak and fleshly, that it has been given,
It is on us that it depends, weak and fleshly,
To make living and to feed and to keep alive in time
Those living words uttered in time. . . .
Fragile as we are, it depends on us whether the eternal Word
Is heard, or is not heard.'[1]

Fr Bouyer says the same thing in his own way, speaking of the complete effacement of the preacher behind the message he is proclaiming. 'It is not by careful polishing of our sermons with pumice that we shall ever succeed [in making them the Word of God]. It will be through their being invaded by Another, who must begin by invading us ourselves.'[2]

Fr Chéry says the same: 'The preacher must be a man of God. What is it the people want? To hear the accents of a heart given to God.'[3]

[1] *Le Porche du mystère de la deuxième vertu.*
[2] 'Prédication et mystère', in *La Maison-Dieu*, No. 16, 1948, IV, p. 22.
[3] H. C. Chéry, *op. cit.*, p. 457.

And the Director of the great seminary at Poitiers: 'The preacher is the living crucible in which there takes place the blending of God's Word and man's word, and his preaching is of value only if he is in profound communion with the mystery of God.'[1]

Fr Roguet sees the secret of an effective ministry of the word to lie in the communication, the shining out of a priestly soul.[2] It seems that on these heights all Christians are one.

But let there be no misunderstanding here. Though the quotations I have made are admirable, though they express in terms that Protestant theologians also might use the mystery of the ministry of the Word, we are dealing here with what is—for the present at any rate—only an *avant-garde* movement in the Roman Church. The authors I have quoted are almost all French. The inquiry needs to be pursued and the same movement studied in the Roman Church in Germany, for example, and in the Anglo-Saxon countries. Would the same be found in Italy? It is true that the Italian ecclesiastical authorities and the Pope himself showed great interest in the Congress of Assisi; a high dignitary of the Curia presided over it, and the encyclical *Mediator Dei*, which was the basis of its deliberations, is an official document of the Holy See. Nevertheless, it was not the speeches by the Italians which left their mark on the congress; it is not Italy which is the leading wing of the Roman Catholic Church; it is much more likely to need to be dragged along in spite of itself. And what of Ireland? what of Spain and Latin America? There were Spanish prelates at Assisi, but no one from Argentina, Colombia or Brazil. These gaps are significant. While there is a reforming and innovating spirit at work in the Roman Catholic Church, there is also a Catholicism that lags behind; one might even speak of a retrograde Catholicism which deliberately retards movement, and which in some respects is still in the age of the Inquisition. It is extremely difficult to speak of Roman Catholicism as a whole, in spite of the magnificent

[1] *La Maison-Dieu*, No. 39, 1954, IV, p. 13.
[2] *La Maison-Dieu*, No. 39, p. 118.

façade of unity which it presents to the world. It is divided and torn by divergent tendencies, some of them the expression of a very high and pure Christian spirituality, others betraying a crabbed and hostile opposition to every innovation, making the slightest reform impossible. I have pointed out the tendencies of what one might call the leading wing of the Church, represented principally by French Catholics. But they are still far from being the whole of French Catholicism. Yet one may greet such signs as a germ and a hope. Will they win the day? Many are doubtful, Roman totalitarianism being what it is. Others cannot help hoping.

VII. THEOLOGICAL FACTORS IN THE LITURGICAL MOVEMENT

Whereas the liturgical movement in the Reformed Church proceeds, as we have seen, largely from a theological revival, and is evolving in close dependence on beliefs about the nature of the Church and of worship, theological considerations have on the contrary played but little part in the present liturgical orientation in the Roman Catholic Church. The movement has been set on foot principally for practical reasons. It was desired to give the Mass new life and a new attraction, bringing the people into active participation in it, instead of allowing it to become merely a spectacle. Such were the determining factors which produced the encyclical *Mediator Dei*.

While the liturgical movement is the child chiefly of pastoral preoccupations, this is not to say that certain more theological factors have not also exercised their influence, especially if we consider less the reforms actually conceded by the hierarchy than the deeply-felt desires of men's hearts as expressed in the resolutions and ideas—some of them quite revolutionary—which have been put forward.

1. The liturgical movement seems to be linked in the Roman Catholic Church with the Biblical revival which the Church is at present undergoing. It is the Biblical revival which is bringing

back the liturgy more and more to the great historical facts of the Gospel, and which is tending to thrust into the background the cult of the saints, in order to concentrate attention on the events in the life of Christ. This new orientation is manifested in particular by the new Order of Holy Week and by the simplification of the rubrics. The decretal *De rubricis ad simpliorem formam redigendis* aimed to restore to the liturgical year its original lineaments by reasserting the importance of the historical cycle of events. From now on the Gospel for Sunday is of greater importance than the commemoration of the martyrs and saints. 'The Sunday rite is gaining ground—Sunday, the backbone of the liturgical year; while that of the saint's-day is giving way.'[1] The purpose was to recall the minds of Christian people once again to the meditation of the mystery of Redemption traced out by the liturgy in the course of the year. It is an attempt, tentative as yet, to disencumber the calendar of its surfeit of saints' days, and to trace more firmly the line that runs from Advent to Whitsuntide, through Christmas, Epiphany, the Sundays of the Passion, Holy Week, Easter and Paschaltide. Christ should not be eclipsed by a multiplicity of saints. 'Doubtless,' writes Fr Doncoeur, 'we shall have to fight against the bid to increase even further the number of feasts (the Sacred Head of Christ, the Queen of the Universe, and so on); and one realizes that sound theology will have to go very deep into the Christian consciousness in order to revive in it an understanding and a love of what is essential in the liturgy.'[2] It is certain that the greater dissemination and deepened knowledge of the Bible have contributed, and will continue to contribute, to the centring of the liturgy more and more on Christ and the history of our salvation.

2. Another source of inspiration of the liturgical movement is the renewed understanding of the nature of the Church as a community of brethren. The same factor has played a part in our case also. It is related to the deepened understanding of the Church

[1] *La Maison-Dieu*, Nos. 47-8, 1956, IV, pp. 303-4.
[2] *La Maison-Dieu*, No. 25, 1951, I, p. 23.

as the Body of Christ, and proceeds from considerations that are exegetical as well as theological. Fr Bouyer makes the point: 'The study carried on within Catholic Action of themes related to the mystical body has resulted in a deeper understanding of the liturgy.'[1] Sociological considerations have also played a part. 'The liturgy,' says Fr Chenu, 'expresses the essentially social nature of man . . . it implies, confirms and consecrates a particular anthropological view.'[2] The development of the community spirit is in fact one of the characteristics of our age, in reaction against the romantic individualism of the nineteenth century. We are tending towards a mass-civilization, in which living shoulder to shoulder is a reality, and even a necessity. Everywhere the social spirit claims its rights. It is, however, a community of a spiritual order that is chiefly meant when the community of the Church is spoken of—a community of prayer, love, and sacrifice. Now, the liturgy is the prayer of the community; it welds together men's souls in the same adoration, the same praise, the same proclamation of faith. The Creed is the profession of faith of the community. The *Gloria* and the *Sanctus* are the triumphal hymns of the community. The Lord's Prayer is the community prayer *par excellence*. The rediscovery of the community, from both the theological and the sociological points of view, lies thus at the root of the liturgical movement, for liturgical prayer is not the prayer of the isolated individual, but the prayer of the Church; it is not a profusion of individual acts, but the single act of the assembled Christian body. The liturgical movement is related to a profounder understanding among many people of the nature of the Church, and at the same time it strengthens the sense of being a community, by valuing liturgical communion above all forms of individual religious life.

3. This realization of the communal character of the Church and of the worship which the Church renders to God is a source

---

[1] *La Maison-Dieu*, No. 25, 1951, I, p. 37.

[2] 'Anthropologie et liturgie', in *La Maison-Dieu*, No. 12, 1947, IV, p. 53.

of new joy. Worship becomes gladness. And doubtless this joyfulness in worship has helped to make the liturgical movement popular. In fact, the liturgy in summing up the essential themes of our faith lays particular stress upon those which are most likely to give rise to Christian joy. How uplifting an experience it is, for example, to sing the *Sanctus* and to render homage to God in one voice with the angels in heaven! Who would not rejoice to share in such a magnificent chorus! Similarly it is desired that the ministry of the word should be joyful, 'preaching by the reborn for the reborn'. Of course the Cross remains, and the preaching of it; but the fact of the Cross takes away nothing from this gladness in worship, for the Cross is our redemption. So it is possible—and how heartily I agree—to speak of 'that Holy Thursday evening, so sad and yet so joyful',[1] and of 'the triumphal atmosphere of Good Friday'.[2] Elsewhere the festive character of the assembly of the community is pointed out. Significant, too, is the increasingly frequent use of the word 'festive' in relation to the Sunday services. Thus, as in Protestantism, the liturgical revival underlines the joyousness of worship and invites us to rejoice. Praise is joy, joy like that of the Poverello of Assisi who one winter's day picked up two sticks, and scraping them together with his numbed fingers as if he were playing a violin, sang aloud under his threadbare cowl: 'Praised be thou, O Lord!'

4. The liturgical movement represents a reaction against a sentimental anthropocentric egotism. It does not pander to men's desires, or the special devotions of this or that individual or section. Its aim is to set the glory of God firmly in the centre once more. 'The liturgy,' writes Fr Doncoeur, 'has as its first and sovereign object the glory of God.'[3] Man is not in the centre of it, with his aspirations and his wants, his states of mind and his scruples. While remaining himself he lives liturgically the life of others; he speaks, acts, and prays as a member of the Body of

[1] *La Maison-Dieu*, Nos. 47-8, 1956, IV, p. 132.
[2] *La Maison-Dieu*, No. 39, 1954, III, p. 130, n.
[3] *La Maison-Dieu*, No. 25, 1951, I, p. 15.

Christ. That is a further source of joy. It is when we remain wrapped up in ourselves, refusing to come out of our shells, that we become a prey to sadness and anguish. But when we forget ourselves, and enter into the life, the praise, the prayer and the song of the community, our sadness is turned into joy.

5. The liturgical movement answers a need for truth and reality. The liturgy is no longer a conventional institution, or a sphere reserved for archaeologists and scholars, or a playground for aesthetes, or mere ceremonial and nothing more. It is alive, the very lungs of the Church, as I have said before. So the fake candles are swept away, people refuse to say evening prayers and commemorations in the morning, and will no longer tolerate that their forms of worship should remain lifeless formulae. Hence the desire to understand, to explain, to avoid making the liturgy a sort of magical incantation; and hence the desire present everywhere to translate the texts and say them in the vernacular.

The new understanding of the Church, the exaltation of the glory of God, the need for truth and authenticity, the liturgical restoration of the history of our redemption—these factors of the liturgical movement in Roman Catholicism are also at work in Protestantism, re-awakening a liturgical sense among the people. There are lines of convergence here which, beside everything that continues to separate us from our Catholic brethren, we are glad to see. In this respect we can associate ourselves with the judgement of Pius XII, when he declared to the Congress of Assisi that the liturgical movement in Catholicism (and, we may add, in Protestantism too) seems 'to be a sign of God's providence for our times, a sign that the Holy Spirit is at work in his Church.'[1]

[1] *La Maison-Dieu*, Nos. 47-8, 1956, IV, p. 330.